Feel It, Heal It, Let It Go

Inspirational Stories, Poems, and Quotes
for Overcoming Mental Health Challenges

By:
Margaret M. Catagnus

Feel It, Heal It, Let It Go - *Inspirational Stories, Poems, and Quotes for Overcoming Mental Health Challenges*

Margaret M. Catagnus

Disclaimer:

For other permissions, please contact the author.
Catagnus, M, (1964)

Feel It, Heal It, Let It Go - inspirational stories, poems, and quotes for overcoming mental health challenges/Margaret Catagnus

ISBN: 978-1-7367702-0-7

Margaret Catagnus
Email: hopepeaceluv38@gmail.com

Cover Photo Credits: Pixabay.com

Dedication and Acknowledgements

With love and respect to my parents, Charles and Margaret Catagnus, who have been my anchor during hard times; my brothers, Charles, Thomas, and Chris; my sisters-in-law, Karen, Kathy, and Holly; my niece and nephews, Michelle Renae, Christopher, Matthew, Patrick, Tommy, and Jordan; and extended family whose love and support have made all the difference in my recovery journey. With deep appreciation to Tom Hagen and his unconditional support, wisdom, and strength. With love and affection to our kitties, Rocky (in spirit), Adrian, and Daisy Mae, who provide joy and comfort during challenging times.

Writing about the impact my mental health struggles have had on my life is something very important to me. My dream to help others is now a reality. I would like to thank my peers, colleagues, therapist, and friends who have encouraged me. Thanks always to Melinda Adams, Marge Anthony, Ellen Bluestone, Kelly Boylan, Leo Boylan Mary Boylan, Terri Boylan, Jodi Bramble, Jim Burgess, Joanna Chodorowska, Linda Debow, Rachel Ellis, Dr. Karen A. Santillo Fiorillo, Barbara Galczyk, Dottie Gannotti, Marla Genova, Annaliese Hagan, Emily Hagan, Joshua Hagan, Dr. Richard Hagan, Patricia Mehl Hanson, Sharon Kachel, Nicole Lewis-Keeber, Dr. Diana Kirschner, Frank Lester, Debra Stella Ludwig, Sheila Haney-Mancini, Yanni Maniates, Beth Michaud, Joanne Moran, Michele Meehan Parr, Peg Pierce, Lisa Schey Rishel, Brian Rothkopf, Dani O'Neill Sales, Paige Jenkins Valentine, Walt Valentine, and Deborah Wolf. Finally, a world of thanks to my therapist of 15 years, Kimberly Vargas LCSW.

Foreword

Mental illness, though more widely acknowledged today than in previous eras, is still subject to a high degree of stigma. People admit to feelings of anxiety or depression but are indifferent to the plight of people suffering from more serious mental health disorders such as schizophrenia or bipolar disorder. Members of society have normalized anxiety and depression, so it is time to eradicate the stigma of mental illness and replace it with a model of support.

The people most capable of bringing about a mindset change are the individuals who suffer from mental illness. If willing to share stories with honesty and candor, people struggling with mental health disorders can help normalize difference and enlighten fellow travelers. The individuals can create camaraderie and generate a community of support.

Reading about the experiences of others facing obstacles faced along the way, the ups and downs of the journey towards healing, and the effective practices have a liberating effect. Reading stories of others who have traversed the thorny path of mental illness brings a vicarious relief and a renewed sense of self. Seeing the strength in others who have worked through their problems and found solutions increases one's own sense of self-respect and self-love.

The spirit of *Feel It, Heal It, Let It Go* is an uplifting collection of stories by people who have found ways to survive and navigate mental illness, heal, let go of their pain, and revel in triumph.

~Ellen Bluestone
The Mobile Professor
https://www.themobileprofessor.com

Table of Contents

Introduction

Dear Fellow Warriors,

You may ask, "Where can I find guidance and comfort during my mental health recovery journey?" During our mental health recovery journeys, we sometimes have many years...or even decades of struggles. Some people experience greater struggles than others. We all have our own unique, personal stories.

The primary goal of the storytellers in *Feel It, Heal It, Let It Go* is to provide hopefulness and inspiration for readers who are still struggling. We hope the authors of the stories, poems, and quotes make you realize *you are not alone*, and recovery does happen!

Warriors experience a roller-coaster of ups and downs from times of wellness to deep darkness. Through *Feel It, Heal It, Let It Go*, the storytellers relate the true weariness associated with highs and lows. The storytellers share their heartfelt emotions during the darkest times; and how they developed and utilized daily coping skills to help bring them "into the light." While the individuals may continue to struggle, the authors reveal their recoveries, which have led them to daily-functioning lives. The co-authors of *Feel It, Heal It, Let It Go* also reveal how *stigma* has affected them throughout their lives. As Mental Health Warriors, we can all do our parts to **crush *stigma***! Are you frustrated with the *stigma* you have witnessed; or have been affected by in your own life? Are you passionate about educating people in society about what *stigma* feels and looks like? If so, *do not give up*. Fight the good fight. Please know: *This* too *shall pass*! Let's get started!

Walking Through the Fear

Overwhelmed with anxiety
Ruminating thoughts
Constant highs and lows…mood swings
Forever thinking when will this end
Fear of the uncertainty
Fear of the unknown
What does the future hold?

The weariness overcomes you
Where to turn…
How can I get off this rollercoaster?
Put in the time, dedication and
Very, very hard work
Every minute, every hour
Of every day
Have patience; this too shall pass

Breakthrough…
Then, The Awakening
Go within searching for peace
Love and serenity
Silence…
Solitude…

Be kind, giving, and loving to others
Faith in Jesus, the Universe,
Higher Power, and
Growth in spirituality
Comes into play

Knowing everything happens for a reason
No coincidences
We are here to fulfill and
Learn our soul's lessons
We are here on earth
With a purpose…
To make the world
A better place than we found it
Call on God, Angels, guides, ancestors
To guide and give you the
Courage, wisdom, and signs of
How to move forward during
times of struggle and times of
GRATITUDE!

Ask and you shall receive
SURRENDER!
All will be well
Namaste

Margaret M. Catagnus

Maggie's Story

I have reflected on my life recently. I recognized signs and red flags from earlier times in my life, indicating anxiety and mood disorders. This is my story.

I was born into the family of Charles and Peggy Catagnus on February 2, 1964. My parents and brothers, Charles, Tom, and Chris were excited to finally welcome a girl into their lives. Our heritage is Italian and Irish. Every Sunday growing up, we enjoyed a tradition of gathering for an Italian family dinner at my grandparents' house. We called our maternal grandparents Mimi and Dadu. My parents, three brothers, my Aunt Ceil, (my mother's sister) and Uncle Dan as well as their children; Sheila, Dani, Franny, and David sat at the table. Dinner consisted of spaghetti, homemade sauce (of course), salad, fresh Italian bread, and always a dessert made from scratch.

Mimi and Dadu had a large yard where all the children could run and play together. Mimi had a beautiful rose garden she adored and we all enjoyed. My brothers, cousins, and I would play wiffleball, croquet, and of course, "Hide the Belt." What is "Hide the Belt", you wonder? To play the game, we would get one of our dad's belts and someone would hide it on the grounds. The other players would try to find it. When someone found the belt, we would run around like wild banshees. If you were tagged by the person with the belt, you "were it!"

Times were different growing up in the sixties and seventies. We were always outside playing some sport or game with friends. Growing up, the children played outside in front of the houses in the neighborhood. Parents didn't worry about us being taken. Childhood days were carefree and good ole' fashioned fun! Our family was active in sports, and we learned about good sportsmanship, fair play, and teamwork.

My oldest brother Charles's sport was football; he played throughout his childhood. A milestone in his athletic career was playing quarterback at Bishop Kenrick High School. Every Friday night under the lights at Roosevelt Field in Norristown, we would attend his games as a family cheering on Charles and the Knights!

In the spring of Charles's senior year at Bishop Kenrick High School, I recall pinning Charles's senior prom boutonniere on his baby blue tuxedo lapel as he prepared to leave with his date whose name was Ann. I recall the look of the 1970s with the ruffled shirts and huge bowties. I did not know what a prom was at the time, but they were a lovely couple as their formal attire matched perfectly. I remember watching them drive away in his teal blue Mustang.

In 1976 when our mom was diagnosed with colon cancer, Charles stepped up to help with the household chores. During the two weeks following our mom's surgery and recovery, Charles assumed the responsibilities of cleaning, doing laundry, and preparing meals. Our mom reduced to 105 pounds when she was in the hospital. I recall Charles helping our mom when she returned from the hospital. I can envision her walking up the pathway slowly with my dad and

Charles. She was dressed in her peach skirt, white blouse, and Espadrille shoes.

Charles really protected me as the youngest and only girl. I remember he bought me a gigantic Teddy bear that was almost as tall as me at the time. He also bought me a "10-speed" Schwinn bicycle with his own money. He worked at Sears in the bicycle and hardware department. He was working his way through Temple University.

My next brother, Tom (whom we called Tommy growing up) was my brother Chris and my babysitter growing up. He would help me in grade school with my reading. I recall one day when the neighborhood kids were outside playing on Pine Street. I was eight years old, and my next-door-neighbor Terry wanted to race me down the sidewalk on our bicycles. My bicycle was broken so I asked Terry's brother if I could use his bicycle, but he said, "No!" I used the bicycle anyway. Racing down the hill, I was winning the race. When I went to put on my brakes, the chain popped. I hit the tree at the bottom of the hill. I don't remember much after that. I do remember my brother Tom coming to my rescue once again. Walking up the hill to our home, I said to Tom, "I can't breathe out of my ear!" He said, "I can't either." We have chuckled about this story over the years. My dad and mom brought me to the hospital, and I had a broken collarbone, which was excruciating.

Tommy was the athletic role model in our family. Tom's sport was basketball undeniably! I recall shooting hoops on our neighbor's homemade backboard when living at our first house on Pine Street. In hindsight, playing in the neighborhood on a makeshift basketball court was the beginning of his illustrious career in basketball. Tommy played as a guard in grade school where Holy Saviour was the division championship team. In high school, Tommy played on the legendary 1976 Bishop Kenrick Catholic League Championship. The Knights faced West Philadelphia High School for the City Championship in March of 1976. I will never forget the dynamite times watching Tommy send the West Philly six-footers in circles as he maneuvered around them making layups to the net. He could really jump! Although the Knights succumbed to West Philly 71-61, it was a game I will never forget.

Tommy ended up ranking as one of the Top 20 highest scorers with 24 points in the Philadelphia City Championship game. He was awarded a basketball scholarship to Philadelphia College of Textiles and Sciences (now Philadelphia University), where he was known for sinking every free throw. One day, he hit 142 free throws in a row! "Practice makes perfect!"

Tommy's discipline practicing dribbling in the basement to shooting hoops for hours influenced me to practice, practice, practice the same way Tommy did. His free throws and sheer determination will never be forgotten by his loyal fans! Tommy was well-known in the Delaware Valley well into his adulthood. I am proud to say "Yes! I am Tommy's little sister!" Sorry, I meant to say "Tom!"

Chris was the older brother closest to my age. We had a cantankerous relationship as children. A story fresh in my mind occurred on Pine Street when I was five and Chris was eight. Chris and I were running up our neighbor's wooden porch steps. Chris fell and got glass in his hand. Although bleeding and in obvious pain, he jumped up like a trooper, and I burst out crying. Chris had gotten hurt and I cried for him... "funny" yet "telling."

At the age of 10, Chris's first sport was football. At the age of seven, I was a cheerleader for his midget football team; The Eagles. During one football game when he was playing for The Eagles, Chris broke his leg. Chris was taken to the hospital where his leg was put in to a cast to heal. Our mom believed Chris would heal completely by lying on the sofa for weeks! After being couch-ridden for several weeks, Chris eventually healed without rehabilitation or physical therapy.

Chris became an all-star pitcher. I remember having catches with him for years at our second home on Locust Street when we were growing up. He would whizz the ball into my glove until it stung. I didn't mind, we laughed about it then, and we still laugh about it as adults. Softball turned out to be my favorite sport. I still tell Chris, "If it weren't for you, I wouldn't be a player." He instilled in me the love for the sport.

At the age of 12, I began lifting weights in the basement. Why? My brother Chris lifted weights, and I wanted to mimic Chris! I was lifting 80 pounds, which was impressive for a 12-year-old girl. Chris was serious about weightlifting. I used to challenge him to arm wrestling, but I could not beat him. When I look at our professional family portraits, I think to myself, "Wow, Chris was really muscular."

Not long after high school, Chris started dating Karen. Chris and Karen were married in 1986. The wedding was beautiful. She looked gorgeous as usual. I was one of the bridesmaids in the wedding party. We wore strapless peach gowns with matching hats. Thinking back, I will never forget what the dress looked like on me with my weight-lifting, swimmer shoulders! OMG! I cringe when looking at the photos! I was far from the thin, petite ballet dancer daughter my mom had hoped I would be. I was more of a tomboy because I mirrored the athleticism of my brothers. Sorry, Mom!

Karen became the kind of sister-in-law who was more like a sister. I could tell her anything and she would still love me no matter what. Karen is the sister I never had. I had known Karen since high school. Her best friend married my brother Chris's best friend, Jimmy. Jimmy is also good friends with my brother Tom.

Jimmy has been part of the family since our early years on Pine Street. I mention Jimmy because growing up, I was the only girl under the age of ten on the block. The other girls were teenagers. I only had boys with whom to play. One summer night, all the neighborhood boys were in our backyard camping with their teepee tents. I sat out front on the step by myself. Jimmy stayed with me, put his arm around my shoulder, and spoke very kindly to me. Jimmy was always nice to me, which meant a great deal to me both as a little girl, and as an adult.

I was an active child and the youngest of four children surrounded by brothers. I befriended a neighbor boy named Jamie, who was a year younger than me. Even among my extended family of eight first cousins; I was one of only three girls. Our neighbors had a homemade basketball hoop where I would spend many days playing with the boys on my street. If there was an activity the boys were playing, I played too. We played wiffleball, dodge ball, ping pong, billiards, and flag football as well as swam and rode bikes. I picked up the rules of the games from my older brothers and their friends.

When I was school age, my mother walked me to my new school, Roosevelt Elementary School for the first day of Kindergarten. As we approached the school building, I saw a fellow Kindergartener on the playground. I distinctly recall a girl who I later found out was named Kathy. She was wearing a light blue jacket, and standing in line to enter the building for our morning class. I was amazed to see someone else like me…chunky. As I remember it now, I realize how strange it was for me as a Kindergartener to have viewed her body as fat. I also made a connection with Kathy because we had something in common even though I did not know her. My mom led me to the door of the school building where I was supposed to follow my classmates and she was supposed to return home. As the other children entered the building, I held tightly onto my mother's hand and cried. When I finally entered the building, I was still inconsolable. My teacher began to play the piano and we sat on the floor and learned the words to the song, "Spoons, Knives, and Forks," I did not sing with the rest of the children; instead, I cried during the whole song.

I entered Holy Saviour Grade Catholic School in first grade. The Religious Sister who taught my class was known to many by her tough reputation; I believed these rumors. I often talked with the twins who were near my spot in the class; third row, fourth seat-even when I should have been quiet. After much scolding, the sister moved me to the front of the room as punishment. I wasn't unhappy about the seat change because I was sitting next to a boy named Peter in my class who I thought was cute!

Even in the first row, I would talk to my classmates during lessons. One day, the Sister scolded me again saying she would throw me out the window if I kept talking. I was so embarrassed, I wet my pants. The children in the class laughed. Showing no regard for my dignity, the Sister gave me paper towels from the lavatory and made me clean up the mess myself. The moment is burned into my memory forever. I spent the entire year in fear of the Sister. Reflecting on childhood memories, I realized my reactions were more than just grade school stress; my nervousness mimicked anxiety. In the 1970s, no term for the feelings I was experiencing existed.

My second-grade teacher was a lay teacher. She was kinder than my teacher the previous year, and she would play the guitar for our class. Inspired by her playing, I began taking guitar lessons. I enjoyed playing the guitar and was good at it, too! I was even selected to play on stage at our school's musical night. I was diligent in my lessons, but during one fateful lesson, I played the wrong chord and the nun pulled my pigtail as punishment for my error. I quit guitar immediately, and have not picked up the instrument since. In hindsight, I realize teachers are influential in a child's development. One strict Nun put an end to my interest in the instrument forever.

The next year was more like the first, my teacher; who was another lay teacher, would discipline students with a steel ruler, and she would slap us across the palms of our hands if we misbehaved. I developed the habit of rolling the bottom right corners of my textbook pages. It was a nervous behavior I developed to cope with my budding anxiety.

Grade school was not all bad though. In fourth grade my teacher was a wonderful woman who would play records for us and lead us in singing all kinds of songs. I remember singing the Disney song "It's A Small World" with her and, as it would turn out, it is indeed a small world. I would reconnect with this teacher many years later into adulthood. In her class, we had many meaningful experiences. On one occasion, she invited students from the Overbook School for the Blind into our classroom. All the students enjoyed the chance to play and learn from people unlike ourselves.

As I entered fifth and sixth grades, my body began changing. As I progressed through puberty, I became increasingly interested in scholastic sports. I signed up for the track team in fifth grade. Shortly thereafter, I remember a man representing Knights of Columbus who spoke to our fifth-grade class regarding a Free Throw Contest being hosted by his organization. The gentleman asked if anyone would like to register. I had been shooting hoops ever since I was six years old, so I registered for the contest in the Age 11 Division. I spent time practicing for the upcoming contest, and on the day of the event, my hard work paid off. I shot 15 out of 20, and won the eleven-year-old group at the local level. Victory advanced me onto the district level resulting in another win, and then onto the city level; yet another victory. The state championship was held at Penn

State University, which was located four hours from our home. My parents, my cousin Missy (who competed in the 12-year-old division), her parents, and I all traveled to the State Free Throw Championship. In the final round of competition, I was up against a petite girl who threw underhand. Despite my best efforts, she beat me by one shot. My 14 out of 20 shots netted me second place and a huge trophy.

My sporting career didn't stop with second place in the state free throw. By sixth grade, I tried out for my school basketball and softball teams. With older brothers to teach me, I excelled in sports quickly. As I mentioned earlier, I would practice grounders and high pops with my brother Chris and when we had time, we would go up to the local baseball fields at Rittenhouse School to practice batting. By the time softball tryouts rolled around, I was ready and I made it onto the team easily. I played shortstop and left field.

During one game, as I was playing left field, I recall feeling disconnected from my body…as if I was observing myself playing softball from outside my body. This experience, as well as sweating under the arms more than most girls my age indicated signs of anxiety. I could characterize what I felt that day as dissociation, a common coping mechanism for people with anxiety. I experienced dissociation throughout my childhood. I have never revealed to anyone my experience in left field or any other times I felt disconnected from my body. I hadn't correlated the significance of the experience to anxiety.

In eighth grade, I played volleyball, basketball, and softball for my school teams. Outside of school, I took tennis lessons, rode my bicycle, and at the swim club and the beach, swam as often as I could. My friends and family called me a fish. Whether at school or at home, I was never sedentary. Although I was active, I was still chunkier than most girls and I was reminded of my weight by my family members. Regardless, I knew I was coordinated and I could run fast. I could still excel in sports. I *did* excel. I was captain of and was named to the All-Star teams in volleyball, basketball, and softball. At the eighth-grade sports banquet, we received our end of the year sports accolades. The banquet was quite the celebration. I won MVP for volleyball and basketball, the Coach's Award for softball, and the Scholastic Award; an award given to a student athlete who played all three sports and maintained good grades. I had convinced my eighth-grade nun to invite a famous football player, Vince Papale to speak and unbeknownst to me, he accepted! During his speech and shaking his hand when awarded my trophies at the sports banquet, I was numb with infatuation. Meeting him was one of the most memorable experiences in my life!

It should come as no surprise to hear I wasn't much of a reader outside of school; instead, I focused on sports. Sports were an instrumental outlet and coping mechanism expending all the nervous, anxious energy in my life! My disinterest in academics was superseded by my interest in sports. I would memorize the answers for my tests rather than retaining and comprehending the material. I could hardly pay attention in class. I realize now my difficulty with academics was likely because of the effect anxiety had on my ability to concentrate. Throughout high school, I was a B- type of student. I always passed, but I wasn't invested in academics the way I was invested in sports and keeping physically active.

My high school experience was coupled with the overarching early signs of anxiety. My underarm sweating outgrew the arm shields my mother would pin into my school uniform blouse. Despite this struggle, I tried out for the JV basketball team and made it. I played guard on our JV team. During our first scrimmage, I went up to catch a rebound and came down hard on my ankle, twisting it. The twist turned out to be more; a hairline fracture that kept me off the court and on crutches. While sidelined with my fractured ankle, my coach told me I should lose 15 pounds. I quit, and never tried out for basketball again.

By senior year in high school, I was working a part-time job and looking into colleges. A co-worker suggested Kutztown University of Pennsylvania. We arranged a visit, I applied, was accepted, and in the fall of 1982, started my freshman year at Kutztown University of Pennsylvania.

Initially, I was taking courses with the intention of becoming a psychologist. I realized immediately I didn't like the courses I was taking. I switched to Special Education, which also did not interest me. My best friend was taking a social work class so I enrolled into the Intro to Social Work course. I absolutely loved it. I changed my major to Social Work. I fit right into the program and I knew I had found my calling in life. I felt at home.

College was my chance to be a free spirit. As an Aquarius, I was always part of different groups, but never a member of a clique.

I was social, but I also enjoyed my solitude. I went on retreats with my Chris House Catholic church community, I made friends in my acting classes, and partied with friends. My closest friends were those I met in my dorm, Berks Hall. I absolutely loved my college experience. I keep in touch with several of my friends from college.

Unlike my experiences from grade school, I can't pinpoint any firm warnings of anxiety from my college days. If anything, I noticed I had difficulty with early morning classes. I rostered for one eight a.m. class, but dropped it very quickly since I had such a hard time waking up in time. Little did I know something life-changing was looming.

In 1984, I spent the summer living and working in Stone Harbor, New Jersey with college friends. My roommate, Terri and I were working in a hotel as chamber maids in Stone Harbor. I recall one day at work after a long night of partying with my friends. When we arrived at work one morning, we were exhausted because we had stayed up all night. We made a conscious decision to nap on the beds in one of the hotel rooms we had just cleaned. After two older co-workers noticed we were missing, they contacted the front desk regarding our unexplained absence. Our nap was quickly interrupted by the owner of the hotel who opened the door with her master key. Let's just say, our employment was terminated immediately.

In the summer of 1985, I lived in Rehoboth Beach, Delaware with other college friends from the Chris House Catholic Community. Their names were Marge, Kerry, and Bill. I worked in the kitchen at a well-known pizza chain called Grotto's making a whopping $4.50

per hour. In the meantime, my roommates were working at The Fruit Bowl making $3.75 per hour. Marge and Kerry left The Fruit Bowl, and joined me at Grotto's Pizza where we worked together the rest of the summer. The mid-1980s summers encompassed some of the best days of my life. Ah, the good ole' days! I will always treasure my college experiences.

While in college in 1986, I accepted a part-time position working weekends and breaks with a Home Healthcare Agency based in Blue Bell, PA and in Allentown. I worked as a home healthcare aide. I worked with aging and disabled adults who needed help with activities of daily living as well as children as a mother's helper.

In May 1987, I graduated with a Bachelor's Degree in Social Work with concentrations in Psychology, Sociology, and Special Education. As a recent college graduate, I moved to Allentown, Pennsylvania, and accepted a job as a counselor for truant male and female teenagers, and sexually abused female teenagers. I was not trained for the position. The counseling program was a last-ditch effort program for these teens. I accepted the job to work with a gentleman I dated in college. I traveled throughout several Pennsylvania counties to counsel the teens. I realized quickly I felt lost in space working with these teenagers. I didn't have any experience with truant kids or knowledge of sexual abuse.

My superiors must have noticed, as they reduced my caseload progressively. I left the counseling program with a handwritten note from my assistant supervisor with the words "Reality Therapy" written on the note. I was confused as to what the note meant, but in retrospect, the assistant supervisor may have identified I was struggling with a mental health issue. I was so disengaged from my life at the time, I didn't yet know what reality therapy meant.

With the help of a social work classmate, in February 1988, I was hired by the Lehigh County Area Agency on Aging as a caseworker. The agency was piloting a program integrating the unsupported deinstitutionalized aging and mental health populations. The department for which I was hired only offered contract work. If the piloted services were successful, the program would be deemed State Civil Service. The new pilot program integrated the aging and chronically mentally ill population. The new demographic population required but were not supported by specialized services. The aging and chronically mentally ill population did not exist until the deinstitutionalization; thus, no programs were in place to meet their needs. Our department was designed to provide the patients the supports they needed to live independent productive lives.

I was not provided with any training encompassing the needs of the aging and mental health populations. My caseload exceeded 85 clients. Of these clients, 15 were intensive cases requiring weekly visits. My co-workers and I successfully passed the Civil Service Exam in preparation for our specialized demographic population to be serviced in Lehigh County.

During the latter part of 1988, I found myself going home occasionally during my lunch hour to lay down to clear my mind. In retrospect, the weight of my work caused me to feel overwhelmed because I was carrying my patients' emotional baggage. One day while working for a client, I expressed my mental fatigue and she allowed me to rest on her couch; which was not professional.

It began on a Wednesday morning on January 27, 1989. Shortly after beginning my workday, I attended a meeting with my co-workers to discuss the confirmation of our department becoming Civil Service for the aging chronically mentally ill population. In the afternoon, I recall having lunch with Kathy, who was a college social work friend. Kathy expressed concern for my well-being.

I have a vague memory of Thursday, January 28, 1989. I returned home from work at night. I spent the evening hanging out with a friend Eric who was my landlord and co-worker at the Area Agency on Aging. When I returned to my second-floor apartment, I put on some music. I had work to do; that night I decided to transform my apartment into a museum. I had delusions of grandeur that I was appointed by Mother Teresa to travel the world as a modern-day Mother Teresa. I was convinced she had chosen me to carry on her mission to help the poverty-stricken individuals throughout the world.

When I finished my work, I fell asleep from 5:00 a.m. to 7:00 a.m. on January 29th. After only two short hours of sleep, I awoke and showered. I put on a pair of blue sweatpants and my favorite expensive fuchsia sweater. I grabbed my volleyball and my briefcase, put on my tennis shoes, and headed out the door.

On my way out of the apartment, I took the morning newspaper resting on the heater outside of my landlord's apartment. January 29, 1989 was an unusually warm day. I set off to visit my group-home clients, I wanted to say goodbye before I traveled the world. I thought everyone knew Mother Teresa had appointed me to carry on her mission, so I did not vocalize my new plans to anyone.

After a round of goodbyes, I took several bags of my clothing to a local shelter. As I drove from place to place that day, I had my car tuned to the radio. It occurred to me that my boyfriend at the time was working with the government to have these radio songs played for me. I visited more clients, issued more goodbyes. As one of my final stops that morning, I visited my office at the Mental Health clinic to say goodbye to my coworkers, Eric and Laura. My coworkers seemed surprised by my appearance, but I knew I didn't have to tell them the news. They already knew, everyone did, I was famous and I was to travel the world with Mother Teresa. I left the office after my goodbyes. Several moments later my pager went off, calling me to the main office in the city of Allentown.

When I arrived at the office, I reported to the secretary, handed in my pager and keys, and followed the secretary's instructions to wait in the conference room. Soon, my supervisor, the executive director, my coworkers, and the secretary joined me in the conference room. They questioned me but I didn't answer; I didn't have to, they already knew who I was and what my mission would be. They questioned me more and I offered vague answers.

A woman wearing a winter hat who I did not recognize entered the room and spoke to me gently. She asked if I would go with her; I complied. I did not know where she was taking me, but I was experiencing intense euphoria. I was experiencing delusions of grandeur. In my mind's eye, I was the person chosen to travel the world with Mother Teresa. The woman in the hat led me out of the office building where people were gathered trying to get a glimpse of me before I began my travels. I later found out the woman in the winter hat was a crisis intervention worker.

I had been taken by ambulance to Muhlenberg Hospital in Bethlehem, Pennsylvania on Friday, January 29, 1989. The ambulance arrived and transported me to the emergency room where I remained for hours. A guard was posted outside my room and another at the desk in the ER. The guard by the desk was my Pop Pop who had come back to life to guard the ER. A nurse came into my room and asked me for a urine sample. I complied and handed her the sample, but she said she needed more. I knew this wasn't the case and I told her so. On my second trip to the bathroom, I flushed my black beads down the toilet. The nurse left and shortly thereafter, a bearded patient came into the ER. The patient who came and went after a few hours was my brother Chris, in disguise.

Later in the day on January 29, 1989, I was transferred by ambulance, but at the time, I did not know where I was going. The building I was taken to was beautifully showcased by antique furniture and a grand spiral staircase in the lobby. I noticed my parents and brother, Charles, were in the beautiful lobby with me. I held onto the notion today was the day I would walk down the grand spiral staircase to finally marry my boyfriend.

The receptionist asked me several questions and I was taken to the fourth floor. The room to which I was taken had an inner door connecting to another room. My boyfriend was surely waiting on the other side of the connecting door; quite the contrary. I did not realize it at the time but on Friday, January 29, 1989, I went to sleep at Pennsylvania Institute in West Philadelphia, PA. I was a patient in a psychiatric hospital. It was here the doctors hoped to get my delusions under control.

My psychosis and delusions of grandeur persisted. I awoke on the first night of my hospitalization and wandered out to the front desk where two men received me. I thought they were my brothers' friends who were there to prepare for my wedding but they were a nurse and psychiatric tech. The men attempted to get me back to bed.

The first several days were a blur. I knew my parents visited me daily. I found out later my psychiatrist had urged my parents not to visit every day, but my mother gave him a piece of her mind and my parents' daily visits continued. To my good fortune, I discovered the hospital had all sorts of activities available for patients including basketball, volleyball, horticulture, ping pong, pottery, music therapy, art therapy, and billiards. I was blessed my first hospital stay was exceptional. The private insurance I bought was great, thank God. My parents' doctor had suggested Pennsylvania Institute in West Philadelphia above all others in the area because it was ranked as one of the Top 10 psychiatric hospitals in the nation.

On the fifth day of my hospitalization, I turned 25. My parents, brothers, and sisters-in-law all came and gathered with a birthday cake for me. We sat around a table in the activity area. My delusions of grandeur and psychosis had dissipated and I had returned to reality. I knew I was in the hospital, and with my family's support, I demanded to be discharged. The hospital discharged me after only 17 days. As I reflect on my experiences leading up to the hospitalization, I don't think I ever felt the stress in my personal and professional life. My parents broke the news to me regarding the loss my job, my two-bedroom apartment, and boyfriend. Everything I had worked so hard to achieve was gone in an instant. The devastation I felt was insurmountable.

Because of my hospitalization, I was not state Civil Service yet, thus my job was not protected. I believe it was the stress from my job that pushed me into psychosis. I think I snapped from the stress of all my clients. I felt an overwhelming anxiety anticipating being Civil Service. I was worried about the demand of being on call nights and weekends, having to make home visits, and possibly committing the chronically mentally ill patients to hospitals during a mental health crisis. I knew the experiences would cause a paradigm shift in my life.

Upon my hospital discharge in mid-February, 1989, I moved home with my parents and grandmother. My mother and I returned to my old apartment to pack up my things. When I re-entered the building, my room was as I had left it; set up like a museum. My mom and I packed my things and my three brothers arrived to move my old furniture out to the street where my belongings would be disposed, which was a devastating loss.

Reflecting on my stay at the Pennsylvania Institute, I remember my psychiatrist saying to me I *might* be manic depressive.

In my head, I only heard "might." I shut down, and refused to hear the rest of the conversation regarding the diagnosis. My doctors sent me home while I was taking strong mood stabilizing medications. I was in denial throughout the experience. *I was supposed to be the social worker...I couldn't be the mental patient.* I was on the WRONG side of the desk!

The days after my discharge at my parents' house were excruciating. My anxiety was severe; I couldn't sit down, couldn't even unload the dishwasher. Eventually, I had suicidal thoughts and contemplating taking many pills. My mother watched me like a hawk. Those days spent in a haze of deep depression and paralyzing anxiety were some of the worst of my life. *I felt like I was in Hell.* Unable to bear the pain any longer, I demanded to go back to the hospital. The doctors readmitted me to Pennsylvania Institute for a two-week stay. My doctors put me on Lithium and an antidepressant. I don't remember much from that stay in 1989. One instance I remember was when I was experiencing anxiety-driven insomnia. One night, I was so anxious I had to sleep in the living room of the unit. Due to my high anxiety, during the middle of night, I crawled to the wastepaper basket and vomited repeatedly. My cruel night nurse scolded me relentlessly while I was throwing up.

By the end of my stay, I was no longer suicidal and I was discharged once again to my parents' house. I continued with my life as best I could without a job. By May 1989, I accepted a position as a job coach for people with developmental disabilities. I was assigned to a girl with a very low IQ and I was responsible for training her how to collect cafeteria trays for the kitchen at the Ford Plant in Lansdale, PA, run the trays through the dishwasher, and wipe tables. My client needed coaching for months; repeating the same instructions continuously. Even after many months of training, she never mastered the skill.

In October 1989 I interacted personally with a male employee at the Ford Plant while working with my client. My behavior was reported to my supervisor. Within hours, my regional manager arrived onsite. She spoke kindly; informing me I was fired. My delusions had returned. In hindsight, somehow my conversation with the male employee led to my immediate dismissal. I had not been taking my medication consistently, and altered my behavior. I believed God made a natural remedy for every ailment so my medication was unnecessary. My medication would not work effectively if not taken as prescribed. It was only a matter of time before I slipped back into mania. I was unemployed again; took time, and recovered. When I was feeling better, I called the Home Health Care Agency I worked for in Allentown while I was I college as well as when I graduated from Kutztown. I knew the Home Health Care Agency would always have clients for me as a contracted worker.

Beginning in 1989, I was stuck in a continuous job spiral. I would fall back into depression and experience a suicidal state of mind. I would lose my job. I would get better and find new work. Many of the jobs less fulfilling than my previous work; desk work, kitchen jobs; none of them lasted. I bounced from job to job. When each failed, I would return to the same Home Health Care Agency with whom I had worked previously.

The cycle of job and sickness went on for several years, and so did my hospitalizations. I learned a great deal from working with a diverse client population through the cases I was assigned from the Home Health Care Agency for whom I worked since college. I took on clients with physical, mental, and developmental disabilities including Dementia, Alzheimer's Disease, Cancer, Multiple Sclerosis, and ALS. I also worked with Hospice patients in their homes. Other settings included clients in assisted living and nursing homes. The work as a home health care provider kept me afloat financially and, to my surprise, taught me a lot about individuals suffering from physical and mental ailments.

I continued to suffer with mood swings. The roller-coaster rides of highs and lows were horrendous. In 1991 when my primary outpatient psychiatrist became seriously ill, I was assigned a new psychiatrist. During our first session, my new psychiatrist bluntly diagnosed me with manic depression, currently known as bipolar disorder. When the reality of the diagnosis hit me, I broke out into tears. I finally realized I was suffering with manic depression.

As I struggled with anxiety and depression, I felt the need to be loved and cared for by men. I have been attracted to and have attracted men from around the world including Afghanistan, England, Egypt, Palestine, Pakistan, and Nigeria. For some reason, international men were attracted to me. I enjoyed learning about new cultures and foods I had never tried before. Most of the culinary experiences were positive.

In 1994, I married a man, and we were together for approximately one year. I decided to leave him for numerous reasons. I needed to get away. A church friend of mine welcomed me into her home and it was there I made up my mind; I needed to move away somewhere. My friend and her family were from Texas and offered to reach out to friends and family still living there to see about work and lodging for me. My friend's mother found a family from her church who needed a live-in nanny for their children. With the details sorted out, I made my plans for a road trip in October 1995 from Pennsylvania to my new home in Texas. I had several friends between Pennsylvania, Florida, and on my way to Texas. I decided to visit some of my friends on my way down south. This trip was as much a chance for me to get away as it was a chance for me to prove to myself I could travel on my own.

My road trip would take me down the east coast from Pennsylvania, through the entire state of Florida, back up to Alabama and Louisiana, and finally, to Texas. In-laws of a friend of mine from Pennsylvania who ran a hotel in Daytona met me at my first stop in Ormond, Florida. They offered me a beach-front room and wonderful southern hospitality.

After a few days, I set off again. I stopped in Melbourne, Florida, for an afternoon to visit with another friend of mine named Bryan. I surprised him on the college campus where he worked. We talked for hours and I hit the road. On my trek to Miami, I experienced horrendous road rage from a man in a white van who was following me. He could see I had Pennsylvania plates and I was by myself. The road rage rattled me, so I exited the highway to settle for the night at a motel in Vero Beach. After a restful night, I set out again for Miami to see a good friend and old college roommate, Lynne. I spent two fantastic weeks with Lynne; relaxing by the pool in her complex, and exploring South Beach in Miami, Florida.

I had a timeline to keep, and I set off again. On my drive to Alabama, I stopped for the night in Gainesville, Florida. The next day I arrived in Mobile, Alabama. I remember the southern food was delightful. My stay in Mobile was short; I stayed two days with a friend from my Pennsylvania church. She lived with two Peruvian children she had adopted.

My final visit before Spring, Texas was New Orleans, Louisiana. I stopped at a visitor's center and found a $40 coupon for a room in the French Quarters. The lobby of the hotel was exquisite; antique furniture with a Mediterranean style. My room had beautiful Dutch Colonial style furniture. After checking in, I set off to explore the Mississippi River. I stopped into the New Orleans Aquarium and saw dozens of fish I hadn't seen before. I walked through an incredible tunnel tank of fish; I took many photos! I liked the stingrays most of all. From the aquarium, I bought a ticket for a steamboat ride down the Mississippi. While on the boat, I struck up a conversation with a talkative woman and her friends. When I asked her where she lived, ironically, she was from North Wales, PA, which was close to where I grew up. She and her friends were in New

Orleans to see the Philadelphia Eagles play the New Orleans Saints. By the end of the conversation, we both remarked how it was such a "small world" to meet someone who lived only 15 minutes away in an entirely different state. In the evening, I strolled through local shops and decided to have a delicious Italian dinner. I left to explore Bourbon Street and experience the atmosphere of French Quarters night life. I stopped to listen to jazz performers on Bourbon Street. It was getting late so I retired to my hotel room. I was anticipating the next day and my long drive to Texas.

The next day before leaving New Orleans and the French Quarters, I had to visit Royal Street. The street was incredible; full of shops selling exquisite handmade jewelry, the likes of which I could hardly describe to my family. There were art galleries everywhere; featuring artists; both new and old. I loved the Colonial art and antiques. I returned to my room, packed my belongings for the final leg of my journey. I drove all day until I reached Texas. The Houston skyline was beautiful. As I neared my destination, I was sidetracked by road construction causing me to detour off the highway. I found a pay phone so I could contact my host family and get directions to their house.

I had no idea what I would find in Texas, yet I couldn't help but feel excited by my journey. I didn't dwell too long on the fact I had uprooted everything to move to a new state and nanny for a family I had never met. When I finally arrived, I felt as if the place itself was upside down. There was a makeshift wall built into one room with bunk beds, creating a semi-private area where I would sleep. The house itself was a mess with clothes thrown everywhere. The surfaces and floor were so cluttered there was hardly any room on them for anything else. I couldn't help but stare at the mess and wonder what exactly I had gotten myself into. I laid down to sleep, but was awakened by the iron gate outside my window, which made a loud clang when people came in and out of the housing complex.

In the morning, my host mother would yell at her children. When they didn't follow her requests, she would scream loudly and slam kitchen cabinets. In the evenings, she would sit with me and unload her anxieties and worries. I made the mistake of telling her on the phone before I came that I had worked as a counselor for troubled children. She told me terrible things about how her husband abused her daughter. I felt more like the family therapist than the family nanny. After two weeks in this messy arrangement, I decided to leave. I phoned my friend Bryan in Melbourne, Florida and he agreed to let me stay with him for a while.

When I arrived in Melbourne, I sought out work with the Miami branch of the National Home Health Care Agency with whom I worked off and on in the past in Pennsylvania. My first case was a live-in assignment with a disagreeable German man. I didn't stay with him long, and asked for a new assignment. The agency placed me with an elderly woman with Dementia. The 24-hour supervision seven days a week with my patient was stressful causing additional anxiety. Because of the stress, I searched in the want ads for a private room to rent on the weekends, and found a room in North Miami.

After a wonderful two-week Christmas trip back to Pennsylvania by plane to see my family, I returned to Miami and took the shuttle to my patient's home. When I arrived, I knocked and knocked, but there was no answer. Finally, my client answered the knocking at her door, but she did not open the door for me. Instead, she refused me entry and offered to call a cab for me. My belongings were all inside her house and I was beside myself trying to figure out how I would get in to pack them up.

Thankfully, I was able to call the man from whom I was renting a room over the weekends. I loaned him my car while I was in Pennsylvania for Christmas, and he agreed to come pick me up. It took him longer to arrive than it should have and I grew increasingly nervous with the situation. Eventually, he did arrive. He had gotten lost on the way.

At my weekend room, I called the Home Health Care Agency I was working for to sort out getting my things back and to find out why my client locked me out. My manager explained my patient accused me of stealing some household items including a blender and a postal scale. The agency could not give me any more cases. To this day, I can't understand why my client would make unfounded accusations. Before I knew it, a police officer and the agency manager arrived at my new living arrangement with my personal belongings from my client's house.

With few other job leads, I called the Pennsylvania branch of my Home Health Care Agency; the branch that had always been a reliable source of work for me. The manager of the Pennsylvania branch assured me if I returned, he would have a case for me. Still, I waited before making any quick decisions. In the middle of January 1996, I was feeling very depressed. I went on a few interviews in Florida, but nothing came of any of them. Finally, I made the decision to move back to Pennsylvania.

At the Pennsylvania branch of my Home Health Care Agency, I received a case at the local state hospital for criminally insane men. It was not glamorous work, but it was steady. I became friends with a few of the workers there, too. When my depression waned, I moved to Philadelphia and allowed a young woman from Nigeria I met through work to stay with me; she needed a place to live after an argument with her family.

I lived in Philadelphia for a year and a half, but I was restless there and finally made the decision to move back to Florida. I left my furniture to my housemate in Philadelphia, and drove to Florida by myself. I found an apartment in Melbourne, Florida. The complex had a pool and sand volleyball court. I was sold. Before arriving in Melbourne, I placed an ad in the Melbourne paper for work as a home health care aide. I set up a voicemail for interested callers to leave messages for me when I arrived at my new apartment. By the time I arrived in Florida, there were at least a dozen messages on the voicemail responding to my ad.

I enjoyed my experience in Melbourne, Florida. I liked going to the pool and hanging out with new friends on my days off. I was working as an in-home healthcare provider, and working overnight for another job. Both jobs fell through, and I began working at a

BBQ Pit making salad bar fixins'. The restaurant had mouse droppings around the bread racks. Why I worked there instead of finding another Home Health Care job, I will never know.

My mom and her friend came to visit me in Florida. We planted flowers in my front yard and enjoyed our time together during the visit. My friend Bryan was the main reason I moved to Florida. I met him at my college best friend's wedding in 1989 in The Poconos. We walked together in the wedding party, and became close. A year after I moved to Melbourne, Bryan transferred to another university out of the area. After he moved, I did not have a reason to stay in Florida. I sold my waterbed and the rest of my furniture to a young local girl. I picked up my things once again and moved back home to live with my parents again at their home in East Norriton.

As you will notice, the constant instability of housing, jobs, and relationships were always changing. I moved almost 20 times in my life. I lost count of all the moves, and had an insurmountable number of jobs. The instability for almost 20 years was exhausting.

When living with my parents for a few months in 1998, I returned to work as a Home Health Care Worker at Home Health Care, my trusty agency. I could always depend on this agency for new clients. The owner knew I was a good caretaker so I always had work as a contracted aide. I could take a new case or not and he would propose other cases to me. It was always my decision if I wanted to take the case. Home Health Care kept me afloat financially for many years.

I received a call from my good friend Ray from Bethlehem, PA whom I met after college and remained close friends for 10 years when living in Allentown. He told me John Glenn was planning to travel for the final time on the Space Shuttle Discovery. Ray was excited about driving to Florida to see the space shuttle liftoff. We drove my car straight through to Florida without stopping. Ray and I took turns driving. I was exhausted when we finally arrived at the motel, which was south of Cape Canaveral.

Ray was annoyed because I wanted to rest upon arrival. He was also upset because I snored and scattered my luggage in different areas of the room. Ray was so angry, he took off; never to be seen again! I never found out what happened to him or how he traveled home. I felt a great sense of loss when Ray left unexpectedly.

I decided to relocate to a smaller motel room for a few days, and then found a townhouse to rent with a middle-aged man in Merritt Island, Florida. While in Merritt Island, I decided to adopt a Shih Tzu mix puppy, and named her Brandy. I found an ad in the local newspaper for a puppy being sold for $50. I adopted her from a family's home in Palm Bay, Florida whose female dog had puppies.

Merritt Island is just south of Cape Canaveral. Witnessing John Glenn's takeoff was a once-in-a-lifetime experience! I captured the experience by taking many photos amongst the crowd. Although alone, I chatted with strangers and engaged in the excitement of this great event! When the Space Shuttle Discovery was due to return, I was working in a group home, and heard a loud boom! The noise sounded like something had crashed into the roof. My co-worker informed me the shuttle was returning, and the noise was called a "Sonic Boom" as the shuttle penetrated the sound barrier. I will never forget the experience!

A few days later, my mom called. She had experienced a mild heart attack. She also informed me she and my dad were separating. While talking to a male friend of mine, he suggested I collect my toys and go home. My intention was to visit home for a short time as we were preparing to ring in the New Year and the year 1999. Once again, I packed "some things" and off I drove up I-95 North to East Norriton, PA.

My parents had moved to Coleston, which was a beautiful neighborhood in East Norriton where my mom always wanted to live. In my haste to leave Florida, I left several items behind. The items included my first softball glove, tennis racket, Christmas decorations my mom had given to me from childhood, newspapers from the John Glenn Space Shuttle Discovery event, and clothing. I had boxes of books at a storage unit. When traveling to PA, I had my puppy Brandy on top of a tote container with a pillow on top so she could see out. I drove straight through to PA without stopping in North or South Carolina since I had my puppy with me. I stopped at rest stops as needed to give Brandy water and food. We stayed at one rest stop for five hours to sleep, and then continued the trek to PA.

I surprised my parents with my arrival on New Year's Eve, December 31, 1998. My mom and dad were not well when I arrived so I decided to stay in PA. The landlord in Florida requested I return for all my belongings or she would dispose of them. I decided not to return for the belongings, regretfully. I shipped my books from the storage unit at a cost of $300.00! I was living on a shoestring budget during all my trips down I-95 South to Florida, and southwest to Texas. I never worried about my car breaking down. As I reminisce about the events, I realize what a predicament I would have encountered if my car had broken down on the highway. My car was a reliable 1994 Toyota Corolla thankfully.

My mom moved out 10 days after my return. My mom left her dog Champ with my dad and me. Brandy and Champ became buddies quickly. Six months after she left, my mother suffered a mild heart attack. She moved back into the house with us for a few months. Brandy and I lived with my dad in Coleston for a little over a year. Shortly thereafter, he sold the house and I moved with my father who had bought a house in Blue Bell, PA.

I needed a plan. From my experiences as a Case Worker in Allentown, I knew exactly what to do to get myself on the system. I wasted no time going to the Department of Public Welfare where I applied for cash assistance and Medicaid. I began receiving monthly payments. In 2000, I applied for Social Security. After several fruitless attempts, I hired a lawyer and finally succeeded. After two years on the waitlist, I found housing through Section Eight. Finding a place to live was challenging; the Housing Authority only offered housing options close to my roots in Norristown, PA, but I did not want to live in the available housing options. In 2003, I found a landlord who would rent a space under Section Eight in Glenside, PA

I finally secured stable housing but I was spiraling in my work life; jumping from job to job, and doctor to doctor. I can't count how many doctors I have had over the years or the different medications I have taken. I felt like I had tried everything. As mentioned earlier, my doctors had prescribed a high dose of Lithium. I took Lithium for about seven years, and never once did a medical professional warn me about the serious nature of kidney damage caused by Lithium. Unbeknownst to me, I was suffering with early stages of kidney disease.

In August 2001, I was experiencing heavy blood clots during menstruation. While at the gynecologist, I had a procedure called a dilation and curettage. On September 10, 2001, the diagnosis was Stage One Uterine Cancer. My mom and oldest brother Charles came to my dad's house to comfort me.

The next morning, I awoke to the phone. My father called stating a plane had flown through one of the Twin Towers in New York City. I turned on the television immediately and the announcer was reporting the tragic event. During her report, the second Twin Tower was hit by another plane. If you were old enough, you realized the magnitude of the horrific events occurring in America. The Twin Towers of the World Trade Center crumbled to the ground as Americans and the rest of the world were devastated. We will never forget where we were when we were informed about the tragedy. Our nation joined hands and hung American flags outside their homes and we became a unified nation supporting each other through tragedy.

Fast forward to October 4, 2001 when I had a complete hysterectomy. I was 37 years old at the time, and devastated. I would never bear a child. I was the babysitter in my neighborhood beginning at age 11 and throughout my life until the age of 41. I remember when my college friend Jennifer said to me, "Marge, you are going to be the mom with all the kids in the back of the station wagon!" I will never forget her statement. Bearing children was a beautiful thought my whole life. With the hysterectomy and the finality of not bearing children, I became suicidal several times over the next few years.

Estrogen was gone from my body. I did not have my ovaries, and was not producing estrogen. My hormones caused erratic mood swings, anger, and suicidal ideation and tendencies. I struggled through the hardest times of my life from 1990 to 2003; second only to the year 1989 when I experienced my first breakdown.

Patti and Michele were my best friends from high school and college. They were still having children. Patti has six children and Michele has five. As much as I was happy for Patti and Michele, I was tragically saddened; the reality of having my own children would never come to fruition. The devastation of not bearing children was deeply rooted in my heart, and I recall crying for years. In retrospect, I realize having children was not meant to be in my lifetime. The reality is exacerbated because now my family members and friends are blessed with grandchildren.

As I reflect on my mental health history since 1989, I realize I could not have raised children with my mental health challenges and diagnoses. I have accepted my role as an aunt, and realize God did not feel I could handle raising children. I have achieved a level of resolution and am okay.

Not long after my hysterectomy in 2001, I joined the YMCA. I started out in the evening participating in an Aqua Aerobics class on Tuesdays and Thursdays taught by a woman named Joanne. I attended faithfully for many years. One Wednesday night at Aqua Jog class while paddling down into the deep end of the pool, I heard Joanne talking to her friend about the gentleman another friend had set her up with on a blind date. The relationship was not working out. I thought to myself, "Hmm, I bet Joanne is my dad's age!" I told my dad about Joanne, and he attended her class as the only male participant. My dad walked alongside Joanne and began talking to her during warmup exercises. He finally asked her out six months later. We still kid our dad about how long it took him to ask out Joanne in 2002. My dad and Joanne have been together ever since, and have a wonderful companionship. Joanne has a second home in Lewes, Delaware so they live in the Delaware house every summer.

My dad has always been part of my life. He is a man of integrity and instilled his values and morals into my life and my brothers' lives. He supported all four of his children by sending them to 12 years of Catholic school. My dad was known for stating an old English Proverb, "You can catch more flies with honey than vinegar." When my dad explained the proverb to me, he said it was better to be polite to others than rude. My dad drove me to all my sporting events and competitions. When I was sick, he was a strong support to me.

His supports included providing pep talks throughout my downtimes, being instrumental in my healing process, and visiting when hospitalized. He and my mom worked with their doctor to secure a bed for me at one of the best psychiatric hospitals in the country. When I was struggling financially due to my instability and depression, my dad financed my housing for one year. He also loaned me money to help me get back on my feet.

As I continued to struggle with my weight issues, I made a conscious decision to make a change. I happened to see a special report on Channel 10 about gastric bypass surgeries by a nationally renowned physician who was being interviewed on the news. While watching the interview, I decided I needed to call my insurance company to make sure I could have the surgery and it would be covered. In early 2005, I scheduled a consultation at University of Pennsylvania with the head gastroenterology surgeon. My surgery was scheduled for September 2005. During my six-weeks of recovery, I drank protein shakes, and then onto soft foods, and six meals a day. The surgery was successful, and after six months, I lost 101 pounds, but I struggled to maintain my new weight. I began to wonder if perhaps my inability to manage my food intake had anything to do with attention deficit.

In 2006, I read an article in a magazine about an agency who was testing for Attention Deficit Disorder (ADD). I thought I might have ADD. The psychiatric agency was in Fort Washington, PA, which was a short drive from Glenside. After being tested, I found out I did not have ADD. I made the decision to switch my therapist to the psychiatric outpatient clinic where I was tested for ADD. The agency was privately run and accepted my insurance.

In February 2006, I was assigned to a licensed social worker in psychotherapy. My psychotherapist helped me initially with my relationships with men and my weight issues. I had only been six months post-gastric bypass surgery. We discussed how I had lost 101 pounds from my highest weight, and how I was night eating since my hysterectomy in 2001.

In 2009, I discussed my personal achievements with my friends from college who encouraged me to join Facebook to reconnect with friends with whom I lost touch. I had no idea what Facebook was all about, but they seemed enthused about it. I decided to give it a try, enjoyed games like Farmtown and Farmville as well as Bejeweled Blitz. I especially enjoyed reconnecting with college, high school, and childhood neighbors as well as children for whom I had babysat when I was younger.

In 2011, I kept seeing an advertisement on Facebook called "Senior People Meet." The site started sending me matches enticing me to look at the matches to learn more about the men. Over the next several months, the matches kept coming. I decided to pay the monthly fee and become a member. I searched, and to my surprise, I found a man who had very nice pictures of one of his children's weddings. He appeared to have a sweet baby face and was a family man so I contacted him with a message. His name was Tom; and he was 48 and I was 47. We communicated back and forth, and eventually shared my phone number with him. When he called, I was watching the Oprah Winfrey finale, and told him I had to call him back. I returned his call and while we were on the phone, he asked me out to dinner.

Our first date was at Ruby Tuesday at the Willow Grove Mall in Willow Grove, PA. Our meal conversation went well, and I could tell he was a gentle, kind man. We walked the mall afterward, and he reached for my hand. Well, I did not like affection in public, and certainly did not feel comfortable. I started to feel weak in the legs, and began sweating. We went to the Food Court where Tom bought me a water ice.

We chatted away and I revealed to him I lived with Bipolar Disorder. By this time in my life, I learned not to tell new people I met until I get to know them, but for some reason I felt comfortable with Tom to share my diagnosis. He did not seem to flinch. I do not think Tom realized exactly what the disorder entailed.

On our second date, Tom showed up at my apartment with three gifts in hand. He was at a festival, and had won a teddy bear, beautiful wooden roses and some other gift I cannot remember. We dated for a few weeks, but I called it quits because I did not think we had enough in common. I still wanted to remain friends. We kept in touch, and he went on a few dates with other women. After two weeks of Tom's failed dates, we reconnected and decided to date each other exclusively.

Tom likes to drive, so we would drive to the beach, Poconos, Bethlehem for Musikfest, and Philadelphia for the Flower Show. Almost every weekend we had a fun excursion planned. After a year into our relationship, we got engaged and he moved in with me in Glenside. Tom did not like the parking situation with the dance studio and Hot Yoga studio beneath our apartment. Tom searched for places but I was resistant to move. Finally, I became more comfortable with the idea of moving and he found a place in Horsham, PA.

We had adopted two rescue kittens named Rocky and Adrian. I was resistant to cats because I was brought up with dogs, but kittens seemed to be our only option in this apartment building. We have moved to a two-bedroom apartment, which is a corner unit with a patio. Tom was happy to have off-street parking. The apartment location is ideal because it is close to the PA Turnpike, Route 309, and Warrington.

Tom is one of my angels and a good-hearted soul. Tom has been through thick and thin with me and always supports my new endeavors. He cheered me on to become a Certified Peer Specialist, which turned out to be a valuable learning experience. Over the past 10 years, Tom has learned about my illness and has hung in there during my struggles. He was the first man who has accepted me for who I am and didn't try to change me. He was also the first man to whom I could cry and he would comfort me and not tell me to stop crying. He was also the first man with whom I could fully heal from my traumas without judgment, but with compassion, and empathy. Tom provided a safe space for me to be myself while healing.

I feel I have helped Tom be a better human being and opened him up to new ideas and ways of looking at things. We have had our share of ups and downs as most couples do in relationships. We have come to realize our views on politics and religion need not be discussed anymore. Tom's encouragement enabled me to grow and heal through Spirituality practices, support groups, and therapy.

My therapist encouraged me to get my resume updated and apply for jobs on CareerBuilder.com. I decided I wanted to work in mental health group homes. I secured a job quickly as a Residential Counselor. The Program Manager and I became very close. I worked as a Residential Counselor from 2007-2011. During my tenure, my supervisor called and asked if I had ever obtained my Peer Specialist (CPS) Certification. My supervisor at the time switched positions within the same agency, and was working at the Outpatient Day Program utilizing her Doctorate in Psychology. During our phone conversation, she informed me she was given an additional assignment to hire two Peer Specialists for the new department. The Peer Specialists would work in the department specializing in Peer Support Employment/Education. She said she would hire me if I obtained my certification.

I immediately contacted the county offices searching for the Montgomery County Peer Specialist Office. I reached Maureen, The Montgomery County Director of Peer Specialists, and she informed me of the next training date, which was approaching quickly. The next morning, the committee would be reviewing applications for candidates to enter the Peer Specialist Training. Maureen emailed the application immediately. I sat laboring for hours at my desk trying to answer the numerous open-ended questions.

When I sent the email with the application, every other page was blank. To insure my application was delivered to the office safely and on time, first thing in the morning, I printed the document, and drove the application to the Montgomery County Human Service Building in Norristown. I arrived at 8:00 a.m. as the building was opening. The committee had planned to review the applications in the morning. I received a call later the same day informing me I had been accepted into the Peer Specialist training program. Applicants were required to be a high school graduate with two years of volunteer work or mental health experience in the field. My qualifications exceeded the minimum requirements. I was blessed to be accepted into this training because it was the only Certified Peer Specialist training class being held on the weekends, which was perfect not interfering with my weekday job. Classes occurred every other week. After I completed the training, I passed both examinations.

Our graduation ceremony was held after the test in the Science Building of Montgomery County Community College. Each graduate of the Certified Peer Specialist program spoke about his or her training experiences and aspirations for working in the community as a Certified Peer Specialist. Recruiters from agencies attended the ceremony. I was fortunate to have a job lined up working with my supervisor in a new Peer Support Department.

All Peer Specialists are required to have experienced mental health challenges. In November 2011, my mental stability was well under control. I was also given the opportunity working as a Certified Peer Specialist. My days of job hopping had ended.

I started my work as a Peer Specialist advocating, supporting, and instilling hope in my peers (clients). I helped them find jobs and/or opportunities to return to school to obtain a GED. I guided some clients to attend a special program at Montgomery County Community College designed for young adults with mental health challenges. The program introduced my clients to college life and provided training to help the students succeed.

The Montgomery County, PA Certified Peer Specialist Program Director was active in the state. She traveled to Harrisburg, PA, and did everything in her power to increase the national recognition of Montgomery County's Certified Peer Specialist program. I was proud and blessed to be a Peer Specialist in Montgomery County. Our county trainings were excellent, and prepared us to become exceptional Certified Peer Specialists. We were taught to serve our peers, help and support them to lead productive, independent lives in the community. My Certified Peer Specialist Employment/Education program had limited the expansion of my skills because it entailed computer work in an office, which I was not fond of. I felt doing general activities and always being in the community was the next step I should take.

My Certified Peer Specialist friend from training named Phyllis and I remained in touch. She worked for an agency with a wonderful reputation. In 2014, I applied, and was hired for the Certified Peer Specialist job immediately. I enjoyed working in the new agency. The company trainings were exceptional. To remain certified, all Certified Peer Specialists were required by the state to acquire 18 hours of credit training annually. Through the trainings, I was very well prepared to succeed as a Peer Specialist.

Many of my peers had serious mental health disorders. I provided them with support and help with various experiences like goal-setting, self-awareness, advocacy, and education of mental health disorders. As a part of the program, I built strong, trusting relationships and shared my recovery story (both struggles and triumphs); with my peers to encourage them to share their own stories and heal.

On one occasion, I noticed an email from website I did not recognize called meetup.com. I opened the email to find a listing for a meditation class in a nearby town. A peer of mine had just moved to that town and I knew she had been trying to learn meditation on her own. I registered both of us for the class. We grew to enjoy the spiritual and social experience of guided meditation immediately. At first, I attended as support for my peer. I realized I was learning as much as she was. My peer grew leaps and bounds during the three years we attended weekly group meditation sessions together. She was in a shell previously and attending the group meditation helped her blossom into a beautiful butterfly. Her social skills improved; she lost 60 pounds, quit smoking, began applying makeup, learned how to use a digital tablet, and began to meet and date men she met online on dating sites.

I truly believe in the effectiveness of peer support. As a Peer Support Specialist, I work with my peers on coping skills to achieve optimal emotional, mental, physical, and spiritual growth. My peers strive to live functional, productive, independent lives in their communities. Peer support has existed for over twenty years and is just now becoming mainstreamed into society. Peer Support Specialists work all over the world. In 2012, I was fortunate to attend an International Association of Peer Supporters (INAPS) conference held in Philadelphia. It was a great training experience to enhance my peer support skills. For me, being a Peer Support Specialist was very gratifying work. Watching my peers grow, learn, and transition into being independent individuals was worth the challenging emotional work expended. INAPS was granted board certification in 2017. Board certification has broadened respect for Peer Support Specialists within the medical and mental health communities.

I persevered doing my best to support and advocate for my peers on their recovery journey. I worked with them to become independent from institutional housing, lead more productive lives, and heal. I worked hard to build a trusting relationship with my peers so they would open up to me in an effort to heal as they shared their heartaches and struggles. Our one-on-one visits included two- to four-hour sessions in the community. As Certified Peer Specialist, we witnessed our peers' daily mental and physical struggles. The emotional energy expended as a Peer Specialist was draining. I was not prepared or trained to leave my work at the front door when I arrived home daily. I am an empath; absorbing the positive and negative energy of others. I invested so much of my own energy, empathy, and compassion. In time, I began to burn out emotionally.

My career as Certified Peer Specialist was part of my life's purpose of giving back to those like myself who struggle with mental health disorders. Working as a Peer Specialist was the most gratifying work I had ever experienced. I stepped away from the field due to emotional burn out. I chose to refocus my career as a Peer Specialist, and returned to work as a self-employed home health care provider. My work in the home healthcare field was a major part of who I was and helped me manage my mother's care.

My mom and I were very close. We got together often and shared laughs and tears. One day she was telling me her legs had given out a few times. We didn't know why at the time. One night in her home, she went to turn off the light before bed, and she fell. My mom managed to crawl to the phone to call her good friend Millie who lived downstairs. Since Millie had a key, Mom asked Millie to call 9-1-1 and unlock her door. My mom was transported to Mercy Suburban Hospital.

Upon arrival, the hospital staff performed a CAT Scan. The results of the CAT scan were read indicating my mom had a brain tumor, which was pressing on the cerebellum of the brain. The cerebellum controls mobility and fine motor skills. My brother Chris and I were at the hospital. Chris and I were devastated our mom had a brain tumor. The doctors had my mom transported by helicopter to Jefferson University Hospital in Philadelphia, PA. After five days, my mom underwent surgery to remove the tumor.

The surgeon showed my brother Tom and me a picture of her brain after surgery, showing approximately one percent of the tumor they could not extract. My mom had a condition after surgery leaving her paralyzed on her left side. We received reports from the doctors she would regain movement. My mom was sent to a rehabilitation center. One day when I was visiting I noticed she could not pick up her cup well using her right hand, which was her good side. I recognized indications my mom may have suffered a stroke on her right side. Two doctors looked at her and assured me she had not suffered a stroke. My mom remained in rehab for a few weeks. We found a nursing facility for her in Dresher, PA. We thought she would be staying in the home for a few weeks, and then return home.

Upon admission, my mom was evaluated by her attending physician. I told the doctor I thought she had suffered a stroke. The doctor concurred, and transported her back immediately to Jefferson for a scan. We were informed the scan was conclusive. As anticipated, my mom did suffer a stroke on her right side. She recovered from the stroke on her right side.

When she returned to the nursing home, in physical therapy she was beginning to gain mobility with her left arm and eventually her left leg. The physical therapy was very good at the nursing home and the therapists pushed her to exercise. She was able to eventually walk across the room in physical therapy. My mom used a walker for stability during physical therapy, but was bound to a wheelchair.

One day when I was visiting, the nurse helped her to the restroom. The nurse took her wheelchair and put it in her room. She had hoped my mom would not try to get back into the wheelchair without assistance. The nurse stepped away for a moment with the intention of returning, but in the meantime, my mom attempted to walk; fell, and broke her hip. My mom had hip surgery and would never walk again. My brothers and I decided the nursing home staff members were negligent, so we sought out another nursing home. Her next nursing home had a mediocre physical therapy center, so my mom only lived there for approximately one year.

In June 2016 while managing my mom's care, I was also feeling stressed. I started experiencing pain in my legs. It became so painful that I needed a cane to walk. The pain was caused by sciatica. Eventually, I went to the ER for the pain. I was given IV fluid because I was slightly dehydrated. Due to my previous stage three kidney disease diagnosis, my kidneys were not releasing the fluids from IV and drinking fluids. Even though I had been off Lithium for 19 years, the damage was done. In 2014, my primary doctor informed me I had advanced to stage three kidney disease with no prior diagnosis. I had been suffering silently with kidney disease for several years. As a result, and with excruciating pain I became swollen in my legs, ankles and feet and my walking worsened.

After a four day stay, I was discharged to my home. While at home, I fell out of the tub onto both my knees. Tom called the ambulance and I was readmitted to the hospital for what would be a 27-day stay. I was still extremely swollen. The hospital performed numerous tests and finally concluded, I had 60% blood clots in my legs and stomach. The doctors performed intervention radiology to blow out the clots but the procedure failed. I was sent to the ICU to recover. I had to stay on my back and couldn't move for two days. After my release from the ICU, I was able to get out of my bed, and I was transferred to a medical surgical floor.

I would sit by the window in my room and listen to music on a CD player Tom bought for me. I would sob daily as I observed the people outside my window going about their daily lives. My dad, brothers, and many friends came to visit to support me. My condition had not improved, the swelling was terrible and I remember wondering if my feet and legs would ever return to normal like the people I saw walking in the parking lot below.

I was instructed by my vascular doctor and hematologist to be as active as possible. I exercised in bed and in the chair until I gained more strength. When I was able, I walked the floor of the hospital numerous times a day. Upon my discharge and when I was feeling stronger, I began more strenuous exercising including swimming.

To keep up with my exercise, I began swimming at the local YMCA. I set goals for myself; by the end of the year I wanted to swim a full mile. In just four months, I met my goal! I was losing weight and making good progress. By the end of the year, I was swimming one and one quarter miles in the pool three times a week. My progress was so good that the clots in my legs dissipated nine months faster than my doctors estimated. My legs, ankles, and feet remained swollen. The doctor explained my veins were damaged and it was unlikely my legs would return to normal.

As I was recovering from my blot clots, we began to research an alternative facility for our mom. We registered our mom for a Catholic nursing home, and she was placed on a waiting list. Her name was selected, but my brothers and I explained to her the facility had been bought out and was not up to the quality of care as with the previous management company. My mom was relentless about moving to the Catholic nursing home. The conditions were terrible! She was abused physically and emotionally. I contacted Aging and Adult Services, Health and Human Administration, Protective Services, and the Ombudsman. A so-called investigation pursued, but no charges were filed.

One day when I was scheduled to meet my mom at a doctor's office, she never arrived. The facility was supposed to be transporting my mom to the doctor's office. I waited and waited, but my mother did not show up. I left the doctor's office, and when I was walking down the long hall to leave, I saw a woman in a wheelchair being pushed by a young man. When I realized it was my mom, I found her with her glasses crooked, the leg of the wheelchair was hanging out, her sweater was off her shoulder, and her hair was disheveled. I tried to communicate with her, but she was not responding clearly. I immediately told the driver to take her to the Emergency Room located in the next building.

My mother was given an MRI, and the doctors informed me she had developed multiple brain tumors diagnosed as malignant. We were told surgery was not an option. We moved her once again to another nursing home. The facility we selected was the nursing home where we originally wanted her to live years previously but she was not accepted. The nursing home was rated five stars. When I arrived at the nursing home in the morning, the Admissions Director recognized me from my previous visit. She sat down and began to complete the paperwork. I was ecstatic my mom was being accepted. Not long after her admission, her case manager informed us she needed Palliative care, and shortly thereafter was placed on hospice. Her mobility had worsened. She had a poor appetite and was rapidly losing weight. We advocated for our mom to the best of our abilities.

Eventually, my mom began having seizures. The seizures stopped temporarily, and we became hopeful. Unfortunately, the seizures returned. My mom experienced continuous seizures and eventually was bedbound. On Friday, November 3, 2017, I received an early morning call from the nursing home telling me my mom had passed away. I went to the nursing home to say good-bye just before the funeral director took her away. I cried, but was relieved and accepting my mom was at peace and no longer suffering. During her final years, she lived in four different nursing homes. The experiences were anxiety-provoking and frustrating for her. My brothers and I were sad to see our mother suffer as she did for the past seven years. We were devastated as we said farewell to our mom.

The next morning, I awoke with a dry hacking cough. I had never experienced such an uncontrollable cough before. I realized I had a bulge in the upper left side of my abdomen. I went to the Emergency Room where I was diagnosed with a hematoma (internal bleeding) and a case of walking pneumonia. I had worn myself down visiting Mom in her final days but didn't realize it.

On a whim, I called a peer from work and she appeared in the ER with a gift for me. She gave me a pair of cardinal earrings designed by my favorite earring company, Silver Forest. I knew then this was the first sign from my mom she was okay. My mother absolutely loved cardinals.

I was admitted to the hospital, and my brothers planned my mom's celebration of life to be held a week later. Every day the team of doctors would come into my room and speak to me. I would remind them about my mother's funeral being on Friday and would ask if I would be discharged in time for her services. The doctors could never give me a straight answer. The Wednesday before the funeral, the doctors drew blood to test for a blood infection. The results would not be available for at least 48 hours. My question was answered; I would miss my mom's funeral. I was upset, but not devastated. My mom was finally at peace; free from suffering and seizures. I was discharged from the hospital on November 27th.

After my mom passed away, I received many signs assuring me of her presence. I went to a few mediums and an angel reader who all provided wonderful messages to me from my mom. I still cry for my mom because my life will never be the same without her. When I talk aloud to my mom, I imagine her with me always as she is our angel watching over my brothers Charles, Tom, Chris, and me.

While managing my mother's palliative care, my career in Home Health Care was reaffirmed. In February 2019, I returned to my career in Home Health Care. I was self-employed with less stress and much better pay. I began working in May 2019 for a wonderful family in Glenside, PA. My patient was a feisty 92-year-old man with great stories to tell. I enjoyed being with him and visiting with his grown sons. I will always remember our great conversations about his life experiences. He always enjoyed a cocktail of whiskey and water promptly at 5:00 p.m., and a nightcap at 8:30 p.m. One morning, my client fell out of bed, and broke his hip. He entered a rehabilitation facility, and then a nursing home; never to return home. It was sad to see him bed-bound, unable to walk, or come home.

My next patient was a woman with mild dementia. She was a lot of fun, and had a contagious laugh. Her memory was failing at the young age of 74. She loved Andrea Bocelli, so I bought a CD player and his CDs, and she was gleeful listening to him sing. I worked with her for a few months until her daughter found it challenging because she needed 24-hour care. My client entered a Memory Care facility where I would take her out for lunch and to socialize. She adapted well in her new environment so my time working with her ended. I enjoy my fulfilling career in the home healthcare field, and am blessed to have the support of my family and friends.

My brother Charles continues to protect me even as an adult. I realized in 2020 how much I mean to my oldest brother. On my 56th birthday, he recalled the story about the day I came home from the hospital with my parents. Charles said, "Tom, Chris, and I were home waiting for you with our grandparents, and I remember the day our parents carried you through the doorway; home to our family." I tell you, I cried and get choked up now just thinking about his sentiment. His kind words touched my heart in a way I will never forget. We remained close through life's challenges. As an adult through all my surgeries and psychiatric hospital stays, I could always count on Charles to visit with a big bag of snacks and reading material for me, and show his genuine concern for my well-being.

In March 2020, COVID-19 struck the world. I was not working for seven months, and was able to collect unemployment. I returned to Home Health Care in October 2020 working for a wonderful family. My good friend had recommended me to the family. My new patient was wonderfully cultured, attending operas in Italy and around the world. My patient enjoyed a rewarding career as a nurse. She was stricken with Alzheimer's Disease, and was admitted to a Memory Care Facility. Being a nurse and the caretaker for so many years, she had difficulty adjusting to being the patient.

During the months of unemployment due to the COVID-19 shutdown, I spent much of my time healing in the peace and quiet with my kitties Adrian and Daisy Mae. I conducted many Spiritual practices; mostly different types of meditation. I cried a lot thinking about my mom and how much I missed her. I would talk out loud to her. I wanted to write a book for a very long time and felt the lockdown was the perfect time, but I was not motivated to write. I did not beat myself up about it, I accepted the time was not right.

In the heart of the pandemic, I met another good friend named Debbie outside on the patio of Panera Bread in Doylestown. I mentioned I wanted to write a book, and she replied, "So do I!" We exchanged stories of the content of our proposed books. My book had already been planned out in my head for the most part. Her book focuses on stories of seeing signs from loved ones after they passed over. I said, "I get signs from my mom." She encouraged me to go home and write my story of signs from my mom. Without hesitation, I wrote and wrote. After our lunch meeting, my friend Debbie told me she immediately went home and put pen to paper. The same day in September 2020, I was inspired to begin crafting my book. And so, it began…I hired a writing coach and my dream of writing a book has come to fruition. I worked tirelessly writing in my free time at work and at home, and my book came to be.

In late October 2020, I found a second job with a family whose mother was also an Alzheimer patient. When I started working with my patient, I knew the income I would earn would exceed my Social Security limit. I wanted desperately to exit Social Security. I felt stable enough mentally due to my spirituality practices and quality years of therapy with my therapist. I was prepared to take the leap back into full-time work.

I called Social Security to tell them I wanted to stop the benefits. The office worker informed me about the 'trial period' which meant I could collect Social Security benefits while working full-time, but would owe the money back to Social Security. I was a nervous wreck working two jobs not knowing if I could manage both and stay well. I was working 58 hours per week between both jobs.

I am blessed and grateful to have worked for wonderful families over the past two years. Being on Social Security for almost

20 years has also been a blessing getting me through my most challenging days while maintaining financial stability. It is a wonderful feeling to be financially independent once again.

*   *   *

I have encountered those who are uncomfortable with people with mental health disorders because they or those close to them have not experienced people with mental health challenges. Sometimes, people don't know what to say when someone reaches out for a listening ear. Many are worried about saying the wrong thing which might make things worse. Stigma from popular cultural representations of people with mental health challenges may create fear of these illnesses. The struggles boil down to fear of the unknown and a lack of knowledge of accessible resources.

For people living with mental health challenges, fear can cause anxiety and frustration. I became angry when trying to share my diagnosis with coworkers or friends and faced silent treatments, and at times, loss of employment. I have suffered lost opportunities because of someone else's fear and unfounded judgment.

Educate your loved ones. Share your story with friends and family who are safe contacts. Take small steps toward breaking down the barriers built up by **stigma**. I learned the hard way. I thought people would not judge me but, *boy*, was I wrong. Looking back, I can recognize instances when I received harsh judgment. My introspection is a result of many years of work becoming aware of this judgment and the damage it caused. Reflecting on those moments, I am saddened by the number of people I thought I could trust with my story who were not worthy of my trust.

I worked hard to process my anger and hurt at these realizations and fortunately, the feelings have dissipated. I have learned to forgive. I learned not to take it personally. I learned to accept I cannot control someone else's reactions. I can only control how I let the reactions affect me. Acceptance makes way for peace. Peace takes time, though. It takes hard work and perseverance, striving day after day for moments of serenity.

Introspection, self-education, and awareness enable me to manage the emotional highs and lows of anxiety and mood disorders. It is challenging to come out on top of mood shifts. I need to rely on my coping skills to help me recalibrate while feeling balanced and grounded again. When I catch my mood shifting, I stop and reflect. I ask myself what just happened, what changed in the environment or my thoughts to cause a negative mood shift. Awareness of the change allows me to replace negative thoughts with positive affirmations. The information could apply to anyone (with an open mind, free of judgment), not only those with mental health disorders.

I have a unique perspective on mental health challenges. My academic, personal, and professional experiences contribute to the phenomenological first-hand experiences in my mental health journey. I thank God for my mental health challenges. Without them, I would not be the empowered, confident, open-minded, strong, courageous, empathetic, and compassionate woman I am today.

Discovering Spirituality

At a friend's gathering, I met Lisa who asked if I wanted to join her afterward at a friend, Joanna's house. Joanna's group is a healing holistic group, so I decided to go. At Joanna's, my spiritual journey first began. Joanna's group was enlightening and uplifting. I had never experienced anything like it. I knew immediately I liked Joanna's session and I wanted to return. Joanna became my holistic nutritionist, tailoring my food to fit my body's needs.

My spiritual practices were growing all the while. I met several people at this meditation group at Soul Spirit Salt Spa, and became close friends with four of them, Beth, Frank, Jim, and Melinda. They started coming to my house once a month to socialize, meditate, and enjoy good food. They mean the world to me. It's wonderful to have like-minded and open-minded spiritual friends. I also met a woman at the guided meditations who taught gentle yoga and performed Reiki on me during private sessions.

Later at a party for Joanna's birthday, I met a woman named Sharon who does sound healing, meditation, and Reiki. I have attended her sessions for three years. The sessions helped relax and keep my anxiety and depression at bay. A friend introduced me to an angel reader after my mother passed away. Subsequently, I have seen mediums and an acupuncturist. The inspiring people have shared positive messages in spirit from my mother and other loved ones who have passed away. Their messages of comfort help me feel connected; assuring me these loved ones are always with me. God and angels are always watching over us. Call on God and your angels and they will guide you. Talk to them and express gratitude in times of struggle. As God's word reminds us, "ask and it will be given to you; seek and you will find; knock and the door will be opened to you."[i] I asked seven years ago and I have received many positive, uplifting people in my life.

If you put out positive energy including thoughts, and actions like kindness, peace, love, generosity, and care for others; positive energy and good things will come right back to you. Put out negative energy and the negative energy will come right back to you; i.e., the Law of Attraction. At times when I find negative energy is coming from someone, I say to myself, "Maggie, do not get angry or resentful, try to go into peace, because their negative energy will go right back to them.

My spiritual practices have helped me grow and move forward in healing mentally, emotionally, physically, and spiritually. I observe these practices daily to help relieve anxiety symptoms, bipolar mood swings, PTSD flashbacks, and ruminating thoughts. Because of my positive spirituality and manifestation, I am in great gratitude for the numerous and unexpected job opportunities from care.com. Several jobs for which I did not apply surfaced.

I am grateful for all which I have been blessed during my lifetime. I am also thankful for Jesus, angels, ancestors, guides and the Universe for placing so many positive and uplifting people and experiences in my life. Spirituality not only raises my vibration, it also anchors and grounds me to relieve my mental health challenges. I cannot fully articulate how spirituality has solidified my healing journey.

"Awakening: Darkness into the Light"

In a cave…no light;
small light appears on a wall

I was in a pool arms opened and spread apart
seeing myself from above, to my surprise, I was thin

As time went on,
a smidge of light began to shine through the ceiling.

The light opening
began to grow bigger and bigger

I was drawn to the light
I ascend towards the light, still inside looking out

I paused…
finally, I took that giant leap forward immersed in the light

I awoke…what a glorious moment of ecstasy
Never looked back!

With the peacefulness and harmonious euphoric feeling
of the warm sun and the beautiful light beams,

I knew I would continue to grow
And move forward in healing higher and higher

It is all part of our soul's divine plan, spread peace and love
Always being in gratitude
Surrender

Margaret M. Catagnus

Stigma: The Uphill Battle

Stigma comes from society's misconception of mental illness. A common misconception pervasive in popular culture and media is people with mental illnesses are violent. Not all mentally ill people are violent. Even so, there are a surprising number of people who live with mental illness. Very few individuals feel safe seeking the help they need because societal misconceptions of mental illness have built up a dangerous stigma around those who suffer these illnesses. Uncontested stigma leads to greater fear when no one will speak out against misconceptions with facts and real experiences.

The average person likely has limited contact with people who suffer from mental illness. If they do have contact, they very likely aren't aware that those individuals have a mental illness. The cycle of fear and uncertainty surrounding mental illness means those living with these illnesses feel unsafe speaking openly about them and those without mental illness do not receive the chance to learn about mental illness in a way that will make it less "scary" to them. Fear and silence perpetuate more fear and silence.

Mass media including television, movies, news outlets, the Internet have long contributed to negative representation of mental illness. News outlets try to explain away the doings of violent criminals by saying they are "mentally ill," television shows sensationalize and dramatize the extremes of some illnesses, making them seem frightening, movies depict villains that heroes deem "mentally unstable," and the Internet provides countless sources of misinformation. Household forms of media and entertainment create an echo chamber that only solidifies the stigma surrounding mental illness. Consumers of media who do not seek out a deeper understanding of mental illness on their own, face little choice *but* to form and reinforce negative associations with mental illness.

For individuals living with mental illness, seeking support from friends, family, and professionals is challenging. Fear of judgment and rejection by family and friends forces many to suffer in silence. In some cultures, mental illness is not "real," and even an accepting family might not take serious steps to find help for their loved one partly because they don't recognize the underlying illness as "real." In other cases, friends and family without much understanding of mental illness outside the negative portrayals they see in popular media might respond harshly, going so far as to cut ties with a mentally ill family member or friend. Individuals with mental illness who want professional help might even believe the negative portrayals themselves and shy away from seeking the much-needed help due to shame and fear. A lack of support at home means never having the opportunity to find the help needed to lessen their suffering and begin their healing.

In everyday life, individuals with mental illness are subjected to insensitive slurs, jokes made in poor taste, and a pervasive linguistic slang that makes words like "crazy" and "insane" commonplace. These behaviors only serve to make the individual with mental illness feel horrible. Those "discovered" as mentally ill suffer verbal abuse, insensitivity and stares as well as discrimination from colleagues, random passersby, and uncaring acquaintances. I did not become aware of how harshly I had experienced such judgment until recently. I was angry and hurt. I have learned to process my feelings and let them go... *Feel It, Heal It, Let It Go.*

Looking back on my journey with mental illness, I can pinpoint moments during which I suffered the harsh effects of discrimination and judgment without knowing exactly *why*. After my first breakdown in 1989, the friends and colleagues with whom I was rather close cut off all lines of communication. Losing the three friends who were closest to me at the time of my first breakdown is one of the hardest losses I've experienced in the last 32 years. One friend even expressed concern about my well-being two days prior to my breakdown. When I was in the hospital psychiatric ward for the first time, she did not reach out or call.

I approached my mental illness with honesty and sincerity, sharing my diagnosis with colleagues at a few past jobs. I trusted them to see beyond the diagnosis to *me* underneath. I learned the hard way I should not have been so quick to trust. Trusted colleagues shared my confidential personal information with my employers, and I lost my job shortly thereafter. I never imagined my diagnosis would cause so much fear. I had never thought about the stigma associated with mental illness and how it might impact my life.

Since learning the truth about the role stigma has played in my life, I have made it one of my missions to contribute personally to end the stigma associated with mental illness. *Feel It, Heal It, Let It Go* is one of my efforts. My hope is to reach an audience of people who may or may not suffer from mental illness allowing the readers to open their minds to the information contained in this book. My goal is to help reveal the challenges of living with mental illness, encourage others to seek support for themselves or a struggling loved one, and be more compassionate. With understanding and compassion, we can eliminate stigma.

Over recent years content creators of media outlets have begun to address mental illness in a constructive and educational manner. News programs feature advocates for people living with mental illness. Television shows are more sensitive with portrayals of mental illness. Movies shift away from "mentally unstable" villains, and educational Internet resources are more prevalent. We are witnessing small steps, but the work is only beginning!

In 2017, experts estimated that "one in ten people globally" live with mental health disorders.[1] The estimate provided by researchers indicating data on mental health is generally uncertain

---

[1] In terms of global population, 10% equates to approximately 792 million people.
Hannah Ritchie and Max Roser, "Mental Health," Our World in Data, January 20, 2018, https://ourworldindata.org/mental-health.
Our World in Data offers a visual overview of research conducted by the *Institute for Health Metrics and Evaluation* in their *Global Burden of Disease* study.

because of how few people seek diagnosis and treatment. The estimate given above reflects medical and epidemiological data available through surveys and statistical modeling.[2] Over time, the prevalence of reported mental health disorders has greatly increased, but researchers suggest that this is a result of increased "awareness, recognition, and treatment" in recent years.[3] The distribution of mental illness by age globally in 2017 remains consistent over all age groups. In 2017, the prevalence of mental health disorders in individuals under the age of 40 measured incrementally higher than individuals over the age of 40.[4] The difference could result from any number of factors including easier access to diagnostic and treatment resources as well as the impact social media has on younger individuals. Regardless of age, social media can take a toll on one's mental health because it often isolates individuals and strips away face-to-face connections. In some cases, the pressure to present one's self as perfect on social media feeds into symptoms of depression and anxiety. Although social media can be a great tool, individuals should be mindful of how much they engage with various platforms and what impact that engagement has on their well-being.

Fortunately, many well-known figures are speaking out. In a 2019 interview with *Daily Show* host, Trevor Noah, Oprah Winfrey

---

2 Ibid.
3 Ibid.
4 Figures references were retrieved using the *Global Burden of Disease* tool. http://ghdx.healthdata.org/gbd-results-tool

talks candidly about her mission to destigmatize mental illness; "doing this [docuseries about mental health with Prince Harry] is a way of helping people to release the shame and stigma [of mental illness] from themselves."[5] Healing comes when people speak openly about their struggles.

If you or someone you know is struggling with mental illness, please seek help. Resources for mental illness and spiritual growth can be found in the back of this book. If you feel comfortable doing so, go to a local support group or seek out help online. Take care of yourself and practice self-love and care. You cannot help others if you are not well yourself. And, don't forget: You matter!

---

5 Winfrey, Oprah. Interview with Trevor Noah. *The Daily Show*. Comedy Central, COM, April 17, 2019.

Thoughts from the Author

- Healing can take years or decades; it is hard work. Keep in mind, your illness is forming who you are today. Your illness will make you stronger.
- I am proud of the person I have become. I have compassion and empathy for anyone who continues to struggle. In life, doing the hard work allows you to become more open-minded and willing to explore new concepts and new experiences. We are all living the same game of life so let's be kind and supportive to each other.
- I live by the phrase, "one for all and all for one." A team supports, encourages, and boosts each other.
- Misery loves company. Stay away from people who drain your energy. Bless and release.
- You are not crazy and you are not alone. Thousands of people have struggles and are living proof *recovery happens*; you can lead a productive life.
- Try to look at the positives. Looking at the positives may be difficult especially during tough times, but, someday, you'll look back and see what God and the Universe were trying to teach you all along.
- Familiarize yourself with the signs indicating when you are feeling badly or your symptoms are acting up. You will be able to shift and implement coping skills or wellness tools to bring you back to a good headspace. Recognizing the signs early will take practice and time as you retrain your brain and experience self-awareness.
- When I start to get annoyed easily, I stop and ask myself what just happened, what triggered me? Was it something in my environment or something in my thoughts? Self-awareness is key to understanding oneself and changing one's behavior.
- Training your mind to switch to positive thoughts when you are going down negative paths takes practice, practice, practice. You must dig in your heels to develop new pathways in your brain.

- Follow your intuition. Feel it in your gut. If something is wrong, believe it.
- Sometimes you need to lighten up, have a sense of humor, and laugh at yourself. Laughter is healing.
- Always be willing to learn and grow. Be open-minded to new concepts, ideas, and perspectives; a whole new world will be open to you.
- I have won my fair share of battles. I have also lost my fair share. No matter the outcome, I always march forward because I have so many lessons to learn during this lifetime.
- Never be afraid to ask questions. I ask questions even when fearful of judgment. I question often and can't be worried how my inquisitive nature is going to appear to others. Not everyone asks questions. I learn and grow by questioning. When I am fearful, I have learned to go inward and ask myself what causes fear.
- I want to learn and grow to move forward. I break down fear and think about why I am fearful.
- Other people's opinions of you are none of your business. It took me a long time to learn that lesson, and I continue to struggle with being judged. Don't take their judgment personally, it's their lack of empathy and compassion, not your issue.
- Sadly, our culture forces us to hide emotion for fear of being looked down upon. Being vulnerable and open (to a safe person in your life) is courageous.
- Shame is prevalent in people. We may have been shamed about our bodies, intelligence, or mental health; ridicule is not ours to own. The person shaming you has the issue. Sometimes people are not even aware of their issues. Shaming people makes people feel powerful.
- The judgments of others regarding mental health can be harsh. Those affected with mental health challenges may not be aware of the judgment of others. Once you wake up and see the harsh judgment, you may feel angry and hurt. It's okay to feel such emotions. Process it. *Feel it. Heal it. Let it Go!*

- Don't feel afraid to share your experiences with others. We relate most easily when we are vulnerable. Let yourself cry. Tears release oxytocin, a chemical to relieve stress.
- People who are negative are called "energy vampires." If you leave someone's company and feel down, wiped out, or worse than before, he or she should not be in your tribe.
- Everyone is an individual traveling his or her path at his or her own pace.
- Try not to judge someone or something you know nothing about. Judging others is not being open-minded.
- You are never alone. Call a hotline or warmlines to speak to 24/7 if you need a listening ear. Select counties have Peer Support lines which are a great resource. I used them frequently over the last few years. No judgment.
- Stop making excuses for unkind people. If someone is emotionally abusive, calls you names, or shames you for your mental illness, you may want to walk away from the relationship. If they aren't enhancing your life, it may be time to say goodbye.
- Be the one who exudes so much positive energy people will want to be around you.
- Live by example; show love and kindness. Bring people into your peace instead of allowing them to drown you emotionally.
- Try to be aware of how often negative thoughts or negative self-talk goes through your mind.
- Walk beside someone and meet them where they are. You will be a bigger help using a positive approach. You will be surprised how much others appreciate your empathy, compassion, and sincere listening ear.
- Do what you want to do; not what others want you to do. Be your own person; an independent thinker. Be free to be you!
- You always deserve to be respected. Don't tolerate anything less. Speak up.
- Are you carrying a grudge or resentment? Heal it and let it go. Forgive not to justify their behavior; forgive because you must show self-love and self-care.

- You don't need to feel shame or justify your behavior. You have your own mind.
- When you catch yourself in self-pity or complaining, be aware and switch immediately to gratitude. Thank God or your higher power for a roof over your head, food, and clothing. Realize you are blessed. Remember the people in the country and the world who do not possess necessities; a growth mindset could change your perspective.
- I am grateful for all with which I have been blessed. I no longer think about what I don't have in life. I am thankful for my blessings.
- Ignoring your pain and suffering will not make it go away magically. Acknowledging the existence of pain and suffering is the first step to improving your mental health.
- If someone does you wrong; you need not take revenge. Let karma work its magic.
- Ask "What am I here to learn?" and "What am I here to teach?"
- Have faith in yourself that you *do* have; the knowledge and ability to help and teach others. We are students of life; always growing, learning, healing, and moving forward.
- Countless numbers of people have wanted to throw in the towel (I was one of them many times), but did not. It was not my time. It is not yours, either.
- Trust your journey. Ups and downs happen to everyone. Acceptance will help you cope.
- What is your purpose here on Earth during your lifetime? Maybe you know and are living out your purpose. If you do not know your purpose, ponder it…God, your higher power, angels, etc. will show you signs.
- Go ahead, pat yourself on the back. In fact, do it as much as possible because you have put in the hard work to heal. You deserve it.
- Yes, healing is hard work but *so* worth it ultimately.
- If you were talking to a friend right now and he or she had the symptoms you have right now, what would you say to them?

Would you put them down or demean them? No, of course not. So, be kind to yourself as you would be towards a friend.

- Your healing journey; bumps in the road and all, will make you stronger, more courageous, and more resilient. Resilience will take you far in life.

- When life knocks you down, no matter how many times, always get back up. Resilience will prevail.

- Reflect on all your down moments for a minute. Now, think about all the times you bounced back.

- When feeling anxious or having ruminating thoughts, I use my coping skills and wellness tools. I text a friend and tell them how grateful I am to have them in my life. My message just may help them have a better day or night. He or she could be struggling, and you can help them cope.

- Negative self-talk, beating yourself up, or telling yourself you are a bad person may occur if you have suffered trauma such as physical, emotional, and/or sexual abuse. Trauma interferes with your self-esteem, self-love, and self-care. Subconsciously or unconsciously, you may think you deserve the suffering because pain may be all you know. Once you become aware, you can begin to change your thought patterns. No one deserves any kind of abuse on any level. No behavior justifies abuse. The abuser has self-esteem issues, which have nothing to do with you. Abusers need someone to hurt to make themselves feel superior.

- You are not going to master your life in one day. Just relax. If it doesn't challenge you, it won't change you.

- Your diet is not only what you eat but what you watch, what you listen to, what you read, and who you hang around with. Be mindful of what you put into your body emotionally, physically, and spiritually.

Karen's Story

Life is not always as it seems. In social media, we see a rosy facade because people rarely post unfavorable photographs or stories of themselves. When we visit a friend's home for a social gathering, the perception of a person's life and surroundings is tidy. We rarely see the back story. We do not see the not-so-perfect photo, hear the vulnerable story, or walk into an untidy home. I would like to share my back story.

As the first born of four children to Francis and Kay from East Norriton, PA, I was the trailblazer. I was a voracious child, and from a young age, very much a night owl. My mother often retells a story of me in my crib at the top of the steps waving goodbye to late evening guests. I guess my fear of missing out (now known as FOMO) started early! My brother Michael was born when I was four years old, my sister Eileen joined the family when I was six years old, and my brother Steve was the fourth born when I was 12 years old. We also had several pets including fish, hermit crabs, hamsters named Pinky and Dinky, and a dog named Betsy (Ross) because the litter of puppies was born on July 7th. My dedicated mom stayed home to raise the four of us, and my hard-working father was active in the Norristown Jaycees organization and a Certified Public Accountant who worked his way up to President of Cinderella Clothing Industries. One of the perks was being the sample size 12, I always had beautiful dresses to wear. My sister and I were always dressed as twins! I hated it then, but looking back, it was adorable! We grew up on Wellington Road in

East Norriton in one of the most amazing neighborhoods you could ever imagine.

I began my schooling at Cole Manor Elementary School where I have a fond memory of being in the "classroom play" *Little Red Riding Hood*!" After Kindergarten, I entered St. Titus Grade School where I enjoyed eight years adventurous years. I met some of my best friends in first grade; one of whom is still a treasured gem in my life. Her name is Linda.

I enjoyed my teachers in grade school, but a few stuck out in my mind. I will never forget the time when my first-grade teacher (who was a Bernadine Nun) would not allow me to use the little girls' room. Within minutes, I wet myself. She made me put my undies on the heater to dry. I was mortified! The same teacher is the main reason for my neat handwriting. When learning how to print, she would walk around the classroom with a ruler in her hand. If we were not forming the letters properly or quickly enough, she would slap our knuckles with the ruler and make us re-write the words until the letters were formulated to her liking.

Most of my other teachers at St. Titus were incredible. I remember a few of my favorites specifically Miss JanFrancisco, Mrs. Peduto, Sister Letitia Marie, and Sister Rose Colette. My Principal was Sister Samuella. Each teacher and principal encouraged me and helped me become a better student and a stronger Catholic.

My parents encouraged me to participate in a variety of activities including dance and cheerleading. In hindsight, my effervescent personality and level of energy was probably one of the reasons my parents encouraged me to participate in so many activities! From a very young age, I cheered for the Norristown Midget Football Teams where my father coached the Packers and Chargers. In fifth grade, I tried out for the St. Titus Cheerleading Squad and made the CYO team coached by Mrs. Petrillo in sixth grade and Mrs. Wynn (my friend Linda's mom) for seventh and eighth grades. In eighth grade, Linda and I were captain and co-captain of our squad. Our team won the Bishop Kenrick Cheerleading Competition. I will never forget standing with one of my best friends as we accepted the trophy. Ironically, a few years ago, my mom was able to snag the actual trophy we won at the competition at an auction!

A few days a week, I danced tap, ballet, and jazz at Coryell Dance Studio, Miss Bobbie's Dance Studio, and The King of Prussia School of Dance. In addition to in-home music lessons, I played the guitar in Hootenannies at Central Schwenkfelder Church with Mrs. Dottie Mayes. On Sundays, I participated in the 10:15 worship band at St. Titus Church with my sister and another lifelong friend, Karen.

I attended the Queen of Prussia Modeling and Charm School under the tutelage of Miss Kaye Grasso. As the opportunities arose, I was a hair model with Renee at my friend's father Mr. Labriola's hair salon Styl-Rama in Norristown. My experiences were diverse and abundant. Each activity helped me become more independent and better at working with people.

I enjoyed the social aspect of school much more than the academic aspect, but achieved good grades. Most of the comments on my report card were positive. The common thread every year was I needed to learn the appropriate situation to be social. Some things never change! As I grew up, one activity was a constant for me…dance! It was a blessing and a curse. Hitting puberty early (age 10) was the curse in dance. Ballerinas needed to maintain a certain figure, and I did not have the skinny flat-chested look like my dance counterparts. I had a muscular, curvy, athletic build.

In seventh grade, my dance teacher told me I needed to lose weight before our June recital to fit into the costume. I stopped eating to adhere to her request. She threatened (jokingly) to duct tape me into the costume. I was determined to fit into the costume. Success! I had met my goal. Hold that thought.

After a wonderful eight years with the same 50 students, I graduated from St. Titus Grade School in 1976. My maternal grandmother was living with us at our house in East Norriton, and we were very close. One evening, my grandmother left home to attend a special Mass in Philadelphia for the Eucharistic Congress, and never returned. I remember her saying "I am going to see our Lord tonight." My grandmother had suffered a massive heart attack. My grandmother's death was the first time in my memory I had ever lost someone close to me.

In the fall of 1976, I entered Bishop Kenrick High School. The next four years were somewhat awkward for me! Along with two other girls, I was selected for the Varsity Cheerleading Squad as a freshman…another blessing and curse. I was thrilled to make the team, but the senior cheerleaders were not as excited. We were harassed and bullied immediately because we "took away three spots from the upper classmen." We were not welcome by all the girls at first, and had to overcome the stress of social mockery, even though we did nothing wrong. We deserved a spot on the squad. The seniors eventually apologized; but, the damage was done, unfortunately.

I survived and thrived in high school participating in various activities. My involvement in extracurricular activities included: Community Service Corps, Mass Committee, Student Council (Homeroom Representative Junior Year and was elected Student Council Officer Secretary Senior Year), played the guitar and sang on Talent Day, and performed in two school plays. In Sophomore Year, my role was the sassy, crotchety pipe-smoking character, Mammy Yocum in *L'il Abner* and as Mimi-Miss Adelaide's Sidekick and a Hot Box Dancer junior year in the stage production of *Guys and* Dolls. I wrote for the school newspaper and was involved on the yearbook committee. My morning duty was working in the Discipline Office with two of the best…Mr. Pauzano and Mr. Smith. I enjoyed most aspects of high school, especially Senior Privileges.

Outside of school, I was employed at the County Seat in Plymouth Meeting Mall as a blue jeans folder, made waffles and ice cream sandwiches at Waffle O's at the Clover Square Mall in Center Square, and worked at Genuardi Supermarkets in West Point, PA as a cashier and in the customer service office. In junior year, I met my boyfriend Tim. Tim coached his younger sister Dawn and my younger sister Eileen's basketball team. He was my around-the-corner and up the street neighbor. Our parents were friends from the Jaycees and Jaycettes organization, and we attended the same church. Tim attended the neighboring public high school. I always thought Tim was handsome, and I would go out of my way to walk past his house when I was visiting my friends in the neighborhood. I had heard through the grapevine he was not seeing anyone, and decided to ask him to my junior prom. He accepted, and our long courtship began. We attended both senior year proms together as well.

In the spring of Junior year, I applied to represent Bishop Kenrick in the 1979-1980 Montgomery County Junior Miss Pageant. I worked with Miss Kaye Grasso as my mentor from Queen of Prussia Modeling and Charm School in King of Prussia, PA preparing for the competition, which was held at Norristown Area High School (where my boyfriend, Tim attended school). Although I did not win, I valued the experience, and to this day, I will never forget the friends I met or the skills I learned from Miss Kaye...especially social etiquette and learning how to "fall gracefully!"

I survived the high school years. It was no surprise to anyone in the senior year Superlatives Section of the 1980 Yearbook *Kenecho,* I received the "Most Active" female senior award along with a boy named Chris (now a Catholic priest) who was voted the "Most Active Male." At our high school graduation at Temple Ambler Campus the student council officers were honored by sitting on stage of the commencement exercises. All the other student government class officers received service awards at graduation except for me. I was hurt especially because I gave Kenrick my all...every day. I learned a valuable lesson from the experience. Although it hurt at the time, my parents taught me the importance of gratitude and acceptance. What had happened was out of my control. I learned it was acceptable to feel rewarded intrinsically, and sometimes even though you are doing a good job, you are not always extrinsically rewarded or acknowledged. I did not grow up in an "everyone wins a trophy environment."

Several teachers and coaches from high school made an impact on my life. My cheerleading coach, Mrs. Alba was tough on her squad. We respected our coach, and wanted to please her. Mrs. Alba raised the bar for me and the other girls on the squad. Senior year football games were the best! I will never forget the many Friday nights under the lights at Roosevelt Stadium cheering on our Green and Gold Knights! We used to throw mini footballs into the stands, and as seniors, we had our names stickered onto our huge green megaphones. Homecoming games were my favorite! We would march in parades with the band and on floats traveling from our high school on Johnson Highway and Old Arch Road to Roosevelt Field. Meeting alumni from our school who attended the game was amazing. I felt like a celebrity on the sidelines representing our amazing school!

Academically, many teachers were role models to me. My passion for grammar and literature was cultivated by my English teachers: Mrs. Roman, Ms. Liebsch, and Ms. Turner. My entrepreneurial spirit was encouraged by my business teachers: Mr. Canney and Mrs. Wahl. I was encouraged to follow my spiritual dreams by my principals Father LaHart and Father Murray. The school secretary, Mrs. Wallin taught me kindness and stewardship as well as multitasking (because SHE was amazing!) I learned the importance of having a sense of humor and individualism from Senor

Amici. His green beard on St. Patrick's Day was always a fan favorite! Mr. Pauzano and Mr. Smith drew me in with their sarcasm and quick wit. I respected both gentlemen who were like fathers to the students at Kenrick *en loco parentis*.

Because of my strong high school exposure to English and Literature, I selected English Literature as my undergraduate degree at my Alma Mater, Rosemont College, which was the perfect school for me. I graduated in a class of 104 strong women who helped mold me into the woman I am today. I had an adventurous four years of college. Like high school, I jumped right in and became involved in as many activities as possible. At Rosemont College, I was a member the Orientation Committee, was Head of House in Kaul Hall Sophomore Year, was a Resident Assistant first semester Junior Year, and wrote for our school newspaper *The Rambler.* I modeled in the Mother/Daughter fashion shows back when the style was "preppy", planned the Father/Daughter Dances, and in senior year, was elected Secretary Year of the Executive Board of Student Government. I was also a member of the Jest and Gesture Drama Club where I performed as Queen Eurydice in the Greek Tragedy, *Antigone.*

In 1983, I struggled with my weight again during a very stressful junior year. I starved myself again. I dropped to an emaciated 90 pounds. I was bulimic this time; all I had left in my stomach was bile. I was sent home from college to gain enough strength to get through finals, and ultimately graduate on time. Fortunately, I bounced back, finished my coursework a semester early, and graduated with a Bachelor's Degree in English Literature. The

teachers who helped me through my tumultuous junior year were Dr.
Bolger, Mr. O'Hara, and Sister Margaret Mary Bell. I was also very
close to the President of the College-Dr. Dorothy Brown, Dean of
Students-Dr. Charlotte Jacobson, and Athletic Director/my Student
Government Advisor-Mrs. Ethel Levenson. My parents and Tim were
also an integral part of my support team during my recovery.

After graduating from Rosemont in 1984, I attended the
Charles Morris Price School of Advertising and Journalism in
Philadelphia, PA on a partial scholarship awarded to me at the Union
League in Philadelphia. CMP was part of the Art Institute of
Philadelphia in Center City. I thoroughly enjoyed my experience in
school during the six-month intensive certification program. Living in
the city was super fun and allowed me to gain much-needed
independence. The worst part of the experience were the roaches who
lived in our apartment on 21st and Chestnut Streets. My roommate
Lisa was from Syocett, Long Island, and we were a good match! I
served as a public relations intern at Greenwald/Christian Advertising
and Public Relations located at 19th and John F. Kennedy Boulevard in
Center City. I enjoyed walking to "work" every day during my six-
month internship. To avoid parking fees, I left my car at Tim's
apartment at Philadelphia College of Osteopathic Medicine (PCOM),
where he was attending medical school, and rode the bus into the city.

After the internship, I worked a few jobs in advertising and
public relations in Philadelphia and Cherry Hill, New Jersey, but I did
not feel as if I had found my piece of sky. In 1987, at the age of 25, I
bought my first townhouse in Sanatoga, PA. Life was stressful again

as my high school sweetheart Tim and I had waited 10 years to get married. I struggled with my eating disorder for the third time, and dropped to 99 pounds. I battled bulimia yet again; this time because of the stress surrounding our wedding. On June 11, 1988, a week after Tim had graduated valiantly from PCOM, we were married at St. Titus Church surrounded by close to 200 family and friends. I had to be sewn into my wedding dress by my mom, Aunt Sally, and Aunt Nancy because the dress no longer fit me.

After the wedding (which was incredible) and reception at Oak Terrace Country Club, we honeymooned for 12 days on the gorgeous islands of Oahu and Maui, Hawaii. Apart from my motion sickness incidences on a rocky boat and helicopter ride, the honeymoon was incredible. The natives welcomed us with open arms! I recall Tim wanting to play golf on Maui, but we had run out of money!

Upon our return, I continued working full-time at Source Finance in King of Prussia, part-time for Genuardi Supermarkets, and was selling Jafra Cosmetics and Skincare products as a side hustle. In the middle of everything, I was also conditioning to audition for the Philadelphia Eagles Cheerleading Squad. In 1988 and 1989, I made it through to the final cut both years, but was not selected. I often wonder how my life would have changed if I had made the squad.

We were blessed with our first son, T. J. in 1989. As a new mom, I re-evaluated my position in corporate America and in 1992, returned to Rosemont College to study for my elementary education teacher certificate. After being guided by positive academic role models in education, the decision to become a teacher was not surprising. In fact, growing up, my parents encouraged me to enter teaching, but I wanted to work in advertising. I finished at Rosemont in two years, and began working immediately. Initially, I worked for a preschool, followed by Computertots, and substitute teaching simultaneously. I had found my calling! I enjoyed touching the future as a teacher, and the classroom was my happy place.

Our son T.J. was known for his knowledge of sports, especially the Phillies! His favorite player was Mickie Morandini. Listening to T.J. say his name was entertaining in and of itself. Being so young and knowing the names and positions of the Phillies always astounded our family and friends! Like his father, Pop Rocky and PopPop Francis, sports were a staple in his life! At the age of three, T.J. began playing soccer in Lower Pottsgrove and played T-ball in our old stomping ground East Norriton. We all enjoyed watching him play! His playful personality drew everyone in! He was adored by his four proud great grandparents and four doting grandparents. When T J. was young, we experienced the losses of Pop Fiorillo at the age of 52 who was stricken with lung cancer and Grandmom Santillo who had succumbed to breast cancer.

T.J. also started playing ice hockey at a young age. I recall a painful memory from one afternoon when he was learning how to skate at the small rink in the back of the King of Prussia Sports Complex. It was a warm summer day, and I had arrived at the cold hockey rink wearing flipflops. When T.J. was coming off the ice, he skated over the top of my foot. At the time, Tim was moonlighting working at Brookside Medical Center in Pottstown, and he called ahead to prep the room so he could stitch my foot. The wound was not too bad indoors in the cold, but when we got outside into the heat, my foot was bleeding profusely. I was in agony! The ride to Pottstown seemed like it took forever to get there. Tim stitched me up immediately, and off we went! The wound ended up getting infected, and took much longer than anticipated to heal. I still have a scar on the top of my foot!

In 1994, Tim, T.J., and I moved into our dream house in Skippack Township. Tim was an up and coming family doctor who had opened his own medical practice in Collegeville. We joined St. Eleanor Parish in Collegeville, PA, and I quickly reunited with a childhood friend from our neighborhood and St. Titus Church. Karen, who was the director of the worship group later named the Spirit Revival Band, asked me to join. Singing and playing the guitar was something I did not realize I had missed! I joined the band immediately to play my guitar, play percussion, and sing.

After substitute teaching in the Perkiomen Valley School District from 1993-1996, and shortly after beginning my Master's work at Rosemont College, I landed a job as the Kindergarten-Grade Eight Computer Coordinator at St. Eleanor School. Although I loved my job and the students at SES, I knew I wanted to earn my Master's Degree, but could not finance my education, so after three years, I began to seek employment opportunities in the local public schools.

Our second son, Christopher (also known as Henry) was born in 1998 during my third year at St. Eleanor School. The week Christopher was born, he made his first trip to the ice hockey rink for T.J.'s practice with the Valley Forge Colonials. T.J. was so proud of his little brother almost nine years his junior. T.J. presented Christopher to his classmates at South Elementary School for his Star Student Show and Tell! Christopher loved watching old "Barney the Purple Dinosaur" and Teletubbies" VCR tapes in a small TV/VCR combo. He also enjoyed playing with his Thomas the Tank Engine trains and singing "The Wheels on the Bus" as I tried to calm him down. When Christopher was irritable, we called him Henry, which was the name of one of the trains from his many videos.

A year after Christopher was born, a former colleague advised me of a posting for a Business Teacher position at Indian Valley Middle School. I interviewed with the school principal, and was offered the job almost immediately. As a Business Teacher, I was able to merge my love for design from my career in advertising and public relations and my entrepreneurial spirit with the strategies and foundations of education.

Four months into the job as a Business Teacher, my father, Francis passed away at the young age of 60 due to kidney failure. Three days before my father passed away on 1/3/2000, we had a heart-to-heart talk in our newly finished basement after he crawled down the steps to see it. We chatted about many topics, but my future was his biggest concern. He asked me when I would finish my Master's Degree, and I told him approximately two years. My dad also asked me if I would ever consider a terminal degree. Of course, I adamantly replied "NO!" He asked me to promise him I would study for my doctorate. How could I let my father down?

As anticipated, in May 2002 after passing the comprehensive exam and writing my action research paper (with my two-year-old son Christopher on my lap), I graduated with a 3.96 GPA and a Master's Degree in Technology in Education. I was the recipient of the Sister Mary Dennis Lynch Award for Excellence in the field of Technology. My father was the angel on my shoulder guiding me to the finish line. My education was reimbursed generously by my school district because I had achieved the required academic average.

Several years passed, and my final chat with my dad haunted me. In 2010, I applied to University of Phoenix, St. Joseph's University, and Drexel University. I decided to pursue my doctorate in Educational Leadership in Technology at University of Phoenix attending school online; why not? From 2009-2011, I had experienced several traumatic events in my life including an unexpected job transfer from middle school to elementary school, and a divorce after a 22-year marriage. You guessed it, my eating disorder flared up once again. My school nurse at Indian Valley was Debbie. She spoke sternly to me about my condition, and referred me to seek help immediately. Within two days, I was admitted into a day treatment program at the Renfrew Center in Radnor, PA. My undiagnosed eating disorder history was uncovered through intense therapy sessions, and a plan to restore my health was instituted.

Every day for 46 days from October 15, 2010 to January 4, 2011, I made it my job to get better. I quickly learned for me, food was medicine, and exercise should not abuse the body. I was not permitted to exercise while a patient at Renfrew because I was an over-exerciser and under-eater. I would push myself to the point of exhaustion burning off far more calories than my intake. I quickly learned life is all about a comfortable balance and moderation.

While a patient at the Renfrew Center, I experienced highs and lows. The support I received was top notch. We were encouraged to participate in group sessions as well as individual sessions with our therapists. I recall one art therapy activity where we disassembled a scale, and created an art project with all the parts. It was liberating and freeing to not see a scale as an object which owned me. Another activity in which we participated was a dress-up box fashion show. We wore our own clothing, but accessorized the outfits with all kinds of wild scarves, jewelry, boas, sunglasses, hats, and makeup. We had fun, and got to play like little girls on dress-up day!

Another art therapy project in which we participated was a vision board. The therapist asked us to separate the poster into a present side and a future side. We cut pictures and words out of magazines to represent our current vision and our future vision. I felt a sense of hope when I completed my poster. I still have it. We also designed a Bucket List including unfinished business in our lives. I kept the bucket list as well, and since leaving Renfrew, I have begun to check off the items I wanted to accomplish. Art therapy was instrumental in my recovery; and one final activity we did while at Renfrew was a trinket box. Using magazines again, we found words which reminded us of our feelings and glued them into the inside of the box and found words which reminded us of our outer feelings, and glued them onto the outside of the box. We used a glaze to seal the words. I also use this box at home to store my small earrings. When I open the box, I see the beauty of the earrings as opposed to the limiting words I had selected in 2010 contained therein.

The therapists were convinced I was stuck in a time in my life when I began to struggle with my eating disorder; the age of 12. The problem was exacerbated because I was teaching middle school at the time of my diagnosis. Every day for the past 12 years, I had been surrounded by children entering the same time in my life where I was "stuck" (according to my therapists.) I refused to take any medication because I did not feel sick. I realize an eating disorder is a mental illness…mind over matter. I did not feel depressed or anxious, I just did not want to eat. When I looked in the mirror, I did not see what everyone else did. Body dysmorphia embodied me.

Every evening, we were required to complete a daily checklist and reflection. We were required to submit the forms and could not enter the center if the forms were incomplete. I would place stickers and smiley faces all over my forms before submitting them in the morning when I checked in. The director quickly caught onto my game, and she threatened to discharge me after only two weeks at the center. The experience did not end well!

The turning point in my healing occurred one morning during check-in. Every morning after breakfast, we would assemble around the large sectional couch and chairs in the group meeting room and discuss how we felt after the meal. The word 'fine' was frowned upon. We were asked if we were 'physically full or emotionally full!' One morning after breakfast, I noticed a familiar face sitting on the couch after breakfast, but I could not place her. During "circle time" as we called morning meeting, the new girl spoke up and said something I will never forget. She said her name and told everyone she was shocked to see one of her role models in the same room. The new girl was a former seventh grade star of mine from Indian Valley. I was speechless. I was embarrassed to be a patient in the same facility as one of my former students. I broke down and realized what I was doing was wrong at so many levels!

The therapists and director analyzed our forms daily, and adjustments to our program occurred because of our answers and food logs. We also met with a nutritionist weekly to make food choices for the upcoming week. It was a big deal to 'graduate' from center-provided meals to making our own choices from takeout selections. We were required to select a meat protein, dairy protein, starch, sugar, and fruit/vegetable to retrain our brains as to what healthy eating and balanced meal looked like. We had buffet days for special occasions because a buffet was a trigger for so many of us who struggled with making food choices. We were also encouraged to try foods out of our comfort zones. I do not eat (or like) chocolate, so one day when we were asked to try brownies, I shut down. Another day, we were given fast food, and I shut down because I did not eat fast food. When I shut down, I was required to drink Boost or Ensure…both were gross!

I recall one morning during my transition to a shortened day when I arrived at Renfrew on the Wednesday before Thanksgiving in 2010. It was not my normal weigh-in day (Thursday) and the center coordinator scooped me up when I arrived and whisked me into the weigh-in room. Our weights were taken blindly. We stood away from the numbers on the scale to not trigger any of us who were motivated by losing weight. As I stepped up on the scale, I staggered; I was light-headed. The director asked me if I had eaten breakfast before coming to the center, and I replied, "No, I was running late today, so I skipped breakfast." She immediately sent me to the kitchen and required me to drink Ensure or Boost. I do not drink (or like) milk products, so Boost was my only option. Boost tasted repulsive! I shut down for the rest of the day because I was not happy.

Occasionally, family therapy sessions were an option. I always had my family's support. My mom was my biggest cheerleader, and basically moved in with me and Christopher to make sure I was making the appropriate food choices in the evening. She attended sessions at the center, and provided a scaffolding for me as I re-entered independent living and cooking for myself. She and Christopher were my lifeline since Tim and I had separated, and T.J. was attending Rutgers University. I have always enjoyed cooking and entertaining, but during my stay at Renfrew, I became less social. I disconnected from all social media for six months, and rarely interacted with anyone outside my home although I never felt alone. My friends from Indian Valley sent me a beautiful fall arrangement and I received cards and messages from students and friends almost every day during my medical leave of absence. The messages and gifts were unexpected, but treasured. I returned to school right after Winter Break in 2011. I now had developed the coping skills to deal with the triggers and symptoms associated with my eating disorder. I felt in control of my recovery.

In May of 2011, I found out I would be transferred to Franconia Elementary School, where I would serve as a Technology Integration Specialist. Although I was sad to leave my Indian Valley Middle School family, switching schools was the best scenario for me. I could start over with a new group of people who did not know anything about me. Before the end of the school year in the spring of 2011, I began my doctoral studies at University of Phoenix. The divorce was finalized in May shortly after I began my coursework. I was focused on completing my coursework efficiently, which I accomplished in three and a half years primarily online. I attended three residencies; two in Reston, VA, and one in Nashville, TN. Studying every night and working full-time teaching every day was exhausting. I had the support of all my friends and family as well as my colleagues. After being guided by my committee chairperson, Dr. Liz Young, and my doctoral committee, on April 13, 2015, I defended my dissertation successfully. My published dissertation is entitled "Guidance Counselor Perceptions of Cyberbullying in a K-12 Environment: An Exploratory Single-Case Study." On September 15, 2015, I not only walked in graduation, but graduated with a 3.98 GPA, spoke before a crowd of 7,500 attendees supported by my family at the Prudential Center in Newark, New Jersey, and received the Student Speaker Award...one of the best days of my life!

For the past six years, I have worked as a middle school Business/Science Technology Engineering and Mathematics (STEM) teacher teaching Digital Literacy to grade six, Introduction to Entrepreneurship to grade seven, and Coding and Web Design to grade eight. I also served as the Yearbook Adviser to an amazing committee of creative and hard-working students at Indian Crest Middle School and was the director of the Talent Show for three years.

In December of 2019, I co-authored an international best-selling book entitled "*Undeterred*" with a colleague from University of Phoenix, Dr. Karen Hills Pruden. In March 2020, I earned my AAAI/ISMA Certification as a Group Fitness and Barre Above Certified Barre Instructor. I work part-time at Rascals Fitness and Whole Body Yoga, where I help others lead a healthy life. In service to my Alma Mater, I serve on the Rosemont College Alumni Board of Directors as President Elect. In support of another childhood friend named Kathy, I serve on the Executive Board of her non-profit organization called Pillars of Light and Love, where I also volunteer as an instructor. Through Pillars, I facilitate a monthly online support group for adults who struggle with eating disorders.

Helping and educating others is my passion. Along with Maggie Catagnus and several other friends across the country, I work as a Market Partner for Modern Nature (Monat Global). My career rank is in the top 3% of the company as Managing Market Builder earned by working with a team of rock stars including Natalie (former student and girl boss), Rayledi (sponsor), Erika, Ellie, Judy, Kate, Jeanine, Sherri, Donna, Michele, Carolyn, Claire, Wendi, Pat, Zach, Becca, Sara, Katherine, and Karen. Our company is a Doral, Florida-based healthy-aging company, which manufactures and distributes plant-based, vegan, sulfate free, cruelty-free, non-toxic lines of haircare, skincare, pet care, junior products, a men's line, and wellness products. Educating others on self-care, and how to look and feel your best is one of my goals. I would be happy to help you as well. My website is www.karenfiorillo.mymonat.com.

I am blessed to have a fantastic relationship with my ex-husband who continues practicing medicine in Conshohocken and is the owner of Bella Derma Laser and Med Spa in Eagleville. Our two sons who are now ages 31 and 23 are successful graduates of Perkiomen Valley High School and Rutgers University, where they each played four years of high school ICSHL ice hockey for the Vikings and Division One Club Ice Hockey for the Scarlet Knights. T.J. played defense, and Christopher was a goalie. They are both working full-time now. T.J. is engaged to his fiancée Brittany who is a teacher as well. We also enjoy life with our rescue cat named Snickers and our family dog named Rex who is a Puggle.

My friends and family are a huge part of my life. Every January for the past seven years (except for 2021 due to the Coronavirus), I have hosted a "Beat the Winter Blues" party at my house. My friends from all parts of my life gather together for an evening of fun, food, fellowship, and A LOT OF BLUE clothing, decorations, lights, foods, drinks, gift exchange/scavenger hunt, loads of laughs and pictures! I would be remiss if I did not mention the big blue stiletto chair and the 'high hat' bonus gift. My father always told me to surround myself with good people and bring joy to others. My mom and I work hard to make sure our guests are welcome and well-fed! My mom's blue deviled eggs are always a hit with the girl tribe! Gathering all my girls together during the doldrums of January is a blast. I enjoy encouraging new friendships within all the groups! The Beat the Winter Blues Party has become an annual tradition, and now that Covid has subsided, we will pick up where we left off in 2020.

I have decided to share my silent suffering and recovery from my eating disorder struggle so others will not have to experience the turmoil I did with an undiagnosed condition spanning most of my adult life. The moral of the story is we should not judge a person for his or her facade, we should always strive to uncover the back story. Dr. Fiorillo may be reached for further comment on Facebook (Karen Santillo Fiorillo) as well as Instagram, Alignable, Twitter, and LinkedIn at kfiorillo818. Karen is available for speaking engagements and workshops as well as private wellness consultations.

~Dr. Karen A. (Santillo) Fiorillo
EdD, Educational Leadership
in Technology
MA, Technology in Education
BA, English Literature
karenfiorillo@comcast.net

Dottie's Story

As a small child I did not feel love from humans, but I felt love from the trees, butterflies, bugs, and birds. I didn't feel like I belonged here. When I was small, I was told by my mom my dad was not allowed to pick me up or show me affection anymore. When I was only three years old, my mother was very mean to me (I learned later she was jealous of me). I began to trust humans less and less. Eventually, I trusted no one at all.

Despite this, I had a nice childhood as far as childhoods go. Yet, at age sixteen, I moved out and got my own apartment. I struggled to stay alive. I was still in high school and I studied hairdressing. My work allowed me to make decent money. In my late teens, I became very depressed; at times, I felt suicidal. Sometimes I would just go out into nature. Nature helped me cope with my depression. I felt like nature would speak to me. Years went by, I married and had two children. I felt like something was missing. I started speaking to God and the Universe, asking questions. I began listening to motivational speakers who talked about spirituality.

I sought and read many books on the topic of spirituality. The authors of the books gave me many of the answers to questions I had been asking for a long time. I started going to spiritual workshops. Everything really began at those workshops; they changed my life (over 20 years ago!). I took a class in Integrated Energy Therapy (IET) by Stephen Thayer. He is known all over the world as a master in his field. IET changes you because it brings out your soul's purpose. The tools I learned from IET had me connect with my being. IET works with the higher self, angels, guides, masters, and ancestors on the other side who want to help you. It is hands-on healing. I work with tuning forks, crystals, and singing bowls.

I studied under Yanni Maniates for seven years. I learned IET from Yanni and became a Master. I took meditation classes with him for three years. I taught IET as well; the part of the course before becoming a Master. After I learned IET, I went home and tried it on myself for 90 days. I couldn't believe the energy emitting from my 95-pound body; evidence of how stuck I was before experiencing IET.

I also became a Reiki master; my soul was jumping for joy. I knew if I ever had depression, it would never take me down again as low as it did when I was younger. I still became mildly depressed from time to time, but never went as low. I had experienced darkness; now I was in the light. Reiki is soft healing, mostly on the physical body, but also heals some of our spirituality. Reiki has its own passive energy that helps physical energy more than anything. It is very effective with trauma related to mental health disorders. Reiki calms down things by putting hands on a body. It is possible to do Reiki on plants, water, food, yourself, pets, and others. My friend had a marble ash tray fall on her foot. I did Reiki on her foot. After my touch, she felt better and was able to stand for three hours the next day without any issue.

I had embarked on something which shifted my energy. I practiced dancing, breathing, yoga, walking in nature, and hugging trees. I would often lay in the grass on my back and look up at the sky to let the universe show me things in the clouds. I would listen to the birds and the sounds of nature; it was such a beautiful thing; Heaven here on earth. I have realized we can find ourselves in deep depression because we are not plugged into the right source. I learned all you must do is plug into the right source. You plug in your cell phone so you can use it. We are not plugged in and charged up with the right energy; instead, we are charged by the wrong source. When plugged into the right source, we can feel like a great bubble of light; we can manifest anything we want especially elimination of our depression.

I get up early in the morning, practice meditation, eat healthy meals, drink plenty of water, do yoga, do deep breathing, recite a mantra for controlling my thoughts, play in the fairy village I created, and do things to make me feel joyful. I play with my cat. I spend time giving *me* what I need so I can do the work I need to do as a healer and serve my clients. I must be in a place of clarity. I practice spiritual rituals so I can have clarity. I don't listen to music during the day. Instead, I speak to God all day and recite my mantras. I try to stay plugged into these good sources all the time. In the same manner we eat three meals a day to feed our bodies, we must also feed our spirituality three times a day. Imagine what we could do if we did! We would totally shift. My suggestion is to try something three times a day and get used to it. Eventually, your body will say, "Let's do some more of that." You will become more intuitive so you can listen to your body and mind as they tell you where to go and what to do.

I own Soul Spirit Salt Spa in Horsham, PA. At my spa, I help clients plug into the light with a soul sanctuary God and I have created together. I wanted my Soul Spirit Salt Spa for a very long time, but I could never afford it; it was never the right time. At the perfect time, I was shown how. In 2019, I moved into my new location. The spa is bigger than my previous location. I spent quite a bit to fix up this new location the way I wanted it. At my spa, I do and teach energy work; the act of working on cellular memories of energy that is layered and stuck emotionally and spiritually within bodies. I am not new to teaching, I have been teaching energy work for 20 years.

Think about your body being a river. If a rock or tree falls into the water, the water becomes blocked and stagnant. We call the experience energy blockage. When you allow your energy to flow freely as an unblocked river, your body will function better physically, mentally, and spiritually. In my experience, individuals with a history of trauma have more blockages...complex, layered blockages.

The spa has salt rooms for salt treatments. During a salt treatment, clients sit in zero-gravity chairs, listen to calming music like ocean sounds, and just veg out. It's common for clients to sneeze during these treatments. Many have said they feel relaxed, have slept better, and the treatments alleviate stress and bronchial issues. Spending 45 minutes in the salt room is equivalent to three days at the beach because energy is going to our cells. The treatments put 84 minerals into the body. Humans are 70% water, so if we breathe in salt air, our skin takes in minerals. Treatments bring out the positive and negative because they calm down our nervous systems. The salt fills us up with negative ions and takes away the positive ions which come from electronics like computers, phones, microwaves, etc. Salt also helps dry up our mucus membranes and is very beneficial to our lungs. It kills pathogens and helps build our immune systems and strengthen our respiratory systems. Treatments draw us to a quiet place, which heals our bodies. People who are stressed and people with mental health disorders like anxiety and depression experience calmness and enhanced mood after having salt treatments.

At my spa, I lead guided meditation every Wednesday night. During each meditation, I ask participants to share their names and where they live. It is a friendly group and we welcome new people to join us. I then lead the group into a meditative state and I leave them there for anywhere between 12 and 23 minutes. As time elapses, I do energy work on the group. Finally, I bring everyone out of the meditative state and encourage participants to share their experiences if they so wish. I've been doing guided meditation for seven years. Overall, spirituality has been a great healing force for others as well as myself. I recommend it to everyone.

~Dottie Gannotti
Owner, Soul Spirit Salt Spa
Horsham, PA
https://www.soulspiritsaltspa.com/
Reiki Master
Certified in Integrated Energy Therapy

Emily's Story

I have struggled with anxiety, depression, obsessive compulsive disorder (OCD), and Bulimia for a good portion of my life. I still have struggles to this day, but I try to use certain tools to overcome them. I think an important part of recovery is understanding why I developed these ailments. Reflecting on my childhood traumas help me understand some of the reasons I am the way that I am. Let me go over some key memories I have and how they coincide with my disorders.

From the time I was a baby, I was forced into beauty pageants. The importance of me winning them up until I was eighteen years old was imperative. I did win most of the pageants. My parents spent their money on a pageant trainer with whom I would work four days a week. When I went through my awkward puberty stage, I did not win as many pageants and everyone was disappointed in me. Beauty defined my self-worth. This is where OCD took over my life.

I grew up in a very small rural town. Both of my parents were hard-working and my sister was my best friend. From an early age, my sister and I endured perilous punishments from my father. For instance, my earliest memory of my father was when I was three years old. I made a concoction of baby powder and water and rubbed the mixture on my closet walls (in retrospect, there was no parental supervision at all during my younger years). When my dad arose from his three-hour nap, he repeatedly spanked me. My mother tried to console me; my anxiety and depression began.

When I was around nine years old, my sister's friend showed up to our house and he forced himself on me. Nothing was done about this and he continued life as normal. Later in life, he harmed three other girls and ended up in jail. My bulimia started.

I am a woman with a college education, a loving husband, and a beautiful daughter. I struggle every day to fight my disorders. I do not think the disorders are something I can suppress; control is the most important part of my recovery. I met my husband when I was 14 years old; he was an amazing support system. I had no idea why he loved me, but he did. I am so thankful he stays by my side through rough times. I now have a daughter. I want her to grow up in the complete opposite way I did. Through my experiences, I feel I have become a better mother and wife. My life now has helped me to understand the experiences instrumental in making me the way I am. I know I am not inherently the sum of my experiences. I feel a sense of power when I reflect on the bad things to have happened to me in my life and see I am not the person I was molded to be. I do not give my experiences power over me. They will not dictate my present and future experiences.

I would say the biggest stigma I have dealt with is anxiety and depression. I have been called crazy and others have talked down to me like I was not strong enough to handle many situations. It is important to educate those people and not let their opinions control your next move. If you do not have control, it's okay! You may have a panic attack here and there, but it is not a bad thing. You are who you are, and we all deal with situations differently. We are human beings; not gods. Just know you are not alone in your ailments or disorders. Reach out to others or find a group of people who can relate to what you are going through. I have learned *I am me*. I may be happy one moment and anxious the next but that is what makes me who I am. Having knowledge of why I am the way I am gives me power! If someone cannot accept you, then he or she is the problem…not you!

I love my flaws, I love my beauty, and I love my body because I love myself. Life is too short to condemn yourself to a life of despair.

~Emily

Rachel's Story

My story begins early, at the age of seven. It was the first day of second grade, the weather was beautifully sunny. I was playing on the playground with my friend, neither of us had a care in the world. Another girl came running over to us. I had noticed her staring me up and down. Before I could even say "Hi," she blurted out, in a tone that seemed like disgust, "What, do you think you're cool wearing that purple dress?" She chuckled to my friend. I stood there silently; I had no response. On the inside, I was cringing with embarrassment and felt as if a dark cloud had come over me. I wanted to run and hide. I remember having thoughts race through my brain like "Why would she say that?" "What did I do to her?" "Does she not like me?" I was torn inside thinking about how happy I was to wear that outfit, wondering why she did not like it. It was a short-sleeved, soft, velvet, purple shirt with a flowy purple skirt covered in flowers I had bought over the weekend with my mom. I felt so pretty in my new outfit and could not wait to wear it on the first day of school. Now decades later, looking back on that day on the playground, my heart breaks for my seven-year-old self. Little did I know, the small moment in time would be the beginning of my lifelong battle with self-love with which I still struggle.

As I grew older, I felt as if I was living a *happy*, *normal* life, which in all reality, I was. I had many friends, an amazing family, and a loving home environment. For the most part, you could say I loved life. Although life was good on the outside, there were moments on the inside where I still felt a dark cloud hovering over me. At times, the cloud made it very difficult to see the light of the sun when I needed it most. At a young age, it was hard to understand why I had such an internal battle emotionally. Everyone in my life loved me and yet, for some reason, I did not love myself. I was not only very sensitive but overly critical of my every action. I constantly worried about what people thought of me. My insecurities always found a way to interfere with my everyday life. I could have the best of days while out and about doing *normal kid stuff,* and then come home and feel the weight of the world on my shoulders. It was as if all the negative thoughts running through my head all day finally caught up with me, and I wanted to explode. I remember numerous times being in my bedroom alone questioning, "Why am I here?" and "What is wrong with me?" I told myself over and over how much I hated myself and did not want to be alive anymore. At the time, I was not aware that these negative, combative thoughts about myself were completely driven by the *ego* and influenced by traumatic feelings I dealt with in the past. In fact, I did not even know what an *ego* was until a few years ago.

Flash forward to high school, I was one of the most liked girls in school. I was known to be kind, charismatic, funny, and pretty. I made friends with everyone. One of my most special and humbling moments was being voted into homecoming court every year and winning homecoming queen my senior year. I even got to be a part of my town's Thanksgiving Day parade. I rode in a fancy car with a crown on top of my head and all. It was a big deal in high school and it was a nice confidence boost that I secretly needed, unbeknownst to everyone. I was captain of my lacrosse team and was awarded MVP by my teammates. It was something I never expected since I was not the best on the team. Still, it was a very proud moment in my life. I had some of my happiest years while in high school but at the same time there was always this sadness inside of me and constant questioning of myself that I could never fully understand.

My family has always been very close and still are to this day. I have three siblings; a sister, two brothers; and two very loving, supporting parents. My sister, brothers, and I always got along for the most part. Of course, we would have the normal sibling quarrels. Although there were only four of us, I sometimes thought of myself as the "middle child" relating to having "middle child syndrome." In all reality, that was not the case but I connected to that term because of how I felt about myself. There were many moments during childhood when I was not very nice to my sister. I was often very bossy and always had to be right while putting her down and hurting her feelings in the process.

As for my relationship with my mom growing up, it was always up and down because of my unpleasant attitude and disrespectful way of treating her. My mother, sister, and I, of course, had so much love for each other but I would take out my anger and strife over my emotions and internalized mental struggle on them, the people closest to me. I remember in some of my darkest times I would be by myself in my bedroom. Being alone with my thoughts was extremely detrimental to my well-being. I hated myself and I did not want to be alive at times. The saddest part was I could not fully comprehend why. I believed my parents just saw me as being a typically defiant child going through a phase. Now that I am more knowledgeable, it was because I was being tormented inside by self-sabotaging thoughts and I did not know how to vocalize and properly express the pain I was feeling.

I was 18 years old and just finishing up my first semester in college when the reality of depression set in. The first couple months of college were amazing. I had awesome friends and a fun and exciting social life. It felt great to finally feel some independence. My classes were easy and overall, I was doing very well; except for my health and fitness class in which I received a failing grade. Much of that grade was based on a swim class, in which I chose not to participate due to my lack of confidence in a bathing suit. I was very disappointed in myself but more ashamed of how I felt about my body. My insecurities were at an all-time high and I could not put on a happy face anymore. I was feeling tormented by depressing thoughts and I knew it was time to pack up and go home before it got any worse. What concerned me even more was my physical state at the time. My stomach was reacting to everything I ate, sometimes leaving me in severe pain, and my weight was fluctuating drastically. I knew something was not right and I needed to be seen by a doctor. I said goodbye to my friends sadly, but at the same time was relieved to leave and start a new chapter in my adult life.

It took a lot of courage and it was a long time coming but I realized it was finally time to reach out and get help. I had finally vocalized to my parents and close family members about what I had been going through all these years…what a relief. Reaching out was not easy, but I knew it was a conversation I needed to have, and I knew I could not be the only one in the world struggling inside. I ended up seeing a family physician and I was diagnosed with clinical depression. After many tests, I found out my stomach issues were caused by irritable bowel syndrome which is a symptom of stress. It was a relief to have answers and more of an understanding of the roller-coaster of mental, emotional, physical stress and pain I was feeling all these years. I also began seeing a therapist which was one of the best decisions I have ever made. Having a professional to confide in truly helped change my life. I believe I was beginning my healing journey and was ready to take steps to finding my happiness.

My doctor had prescribed a medication to help with my depression and anxiety. Without getting into too much detail, I tried many different medications. Some worked for by putting my mind and body at ease for a short time, which was a nice feeling, but it wouldn't always last. Another medicine I took made me feel unlike myself because of the possible common side effects. Trying to find the right medicine for me was not an easy process and I eventually became exhausted with the ordeal. Because I was an adult and could make choices that I believed were in my best interest, I decided to explore a different healing route; medicine-free. I absolutely do not suggest this for just anyone. I am not at all against taking medications for mental illness, in fact, finding the right medication could save a life. I was ready to navigate a new way of healing before giving medication another chance.

In my twenties, my life started taking the most eye-opening and beautiful turn. Yes, of course depression and anxiety were still lingering but this is where my journey of self-love truly began. My youngest brother, Jacob, was on a spiritual journey of his own. I was introduced to the practice of yoga. He had just finished his 300-hour teacher training and I was more than happy to help support him and come to a class. I remember entering the yoga center and feeling an instant sense of relaxation. The lights were a golden hue and a peaceful energy existed; not only in the room itself, but radiated from the people around me. I was nervous because it was my first time but everyone there welcomed me with open arms. My first class was amazing! Although I was not in the best shape physically, the practice of breathing through each movement helped to calm my mind and put my body at ease. It was the first time my thoughts paused, and I felt a sense of nirvana.

When the class ended, my brother introduced me to his instructor who was the owner of a yoga center. She embraced me with a big warm hug. I felt comfortable with her immediately, enough to just spill out everything I was struggling with in life. She mentioned knowing several people dealing with similar issues. She said, "That's why we have yoga centers…to get the issues out of your tissues!" Her message stuck with me. I returned the following week and the instructor asked me to be a part of the 200-hour yoga teacher training starting immediately. I was intimidated by the request. I had neither the money to join nor a plan to become a yoga teacher. She told me to not worry about the money right now; we would work it out and to not worry about becoming a teacher. Whether or not I became a teacher in the end did not matter; she felt the yoga training was the leap I needed to help find the love for myself I was always missing. It was time to break free from my little comfort bubble! I never imagined saying "yes" to the yoga instructor would change my life forever, and guide me to becoming the woman I am today.

The most common definition of the word yoga is "the union of mind, body, and spirit." At the end of the yoga training, I was asked how I would define "my yoga." For me, "it is the practice of obtaining a deeper love and appreciation for my inner self (soul) and outer self (body)." I came to realize there is never just one answer to healing oneself, nor is there a right or wrong way. If my heart is in the right place and I put in the necessary self-work, the wounds will heal. I learned to be patient in all aspects of life and to treat myself with nothing but kindness and compassion. Self-love is not always easy because talking down to myself had become a horrible habit after so many years. I try my best to replace negative thoughts with positive ones. I am not my thoughts and I finally had the power to change those habits. When my mind begins self-sabotaging, I notice it, take a deep breath, and let it go. I would not want anyone to treat me with disrespect nor would I want to disrespect anyone else, so why continue to be disrespectful to my own self? I realized how much energy I was wasting letting negative thoughts control my life, and I now had the proper tools to continue living through love and not through hate.

Three of the most important wellness tools I use are what I call the Three "M"s: Mindful, Meditation, and Movement. Mindful is always being aware of what I think, say, or act. Meditation is sitting with my breath and allowing my mind and body to be calm. Movement is the act of moving your body in some sort of physical activity. Along with having a well-balanced diet, the Three "M"s are a pillar to maintaining my healthy well-being mentally, emotionally, physically, and spiritually. I am now living my life in a more peaceful state of mind rather than a stressed state of mind. Not only did my relationships with the people around me get better but my newfound relationship with myself flourishes with love.

During yoga teacher training, I would hear about a life altering moment called a "Spiritual Awakening" or "Spiritual Enlightenment." I did not recognize initially, but was experiencing a powerful yet beautiful self-transformation and realization right before my eyes. I was finally experiencing life rather than just going through the motions. Welcoming spirit into my life was welcoming love into my heart. I learned the difference between hoping for things to change and having the faith that things will change. Life will always have ups and downs; highs and lows, because that is life!

I am now in my thirties and still to this day struggle with depression and anxiety, but I know I must continue to put in the work. I have an abundance of wellness tools and support to get me through. My journey of self-love has been a long and difficult road but it does get easier. I am never going to give up because I am worth it. I am stronger than I have ever been thanks to my lived experiences. Depression does not define me; it has helped make me who I am today and I am so proud to profess it. My healing journey thus far has brought so many amazing, loving, supportive people into my life. I hope by offering a glimpse into my mental health journey, I can shine a light of hope into someone's darkness. The light inside me, which once seemed so dim is now shining with love from within!

~Rachel Ellis
Certified Yoga Instructor
Certified in Integrated Energy Therapy
Rachelsellis353@gmail.com

~Rachel's Poems~

I just want it to be Over

I just want it to be over
The sadness and the bad
The emptiness I feel inside, that I wish I never had
I am tired of always questioning, how did I get here and why
I feel like every night of summer has ended in a cry
I just want it to be over
The hurt and all of the sorrow
I deserve to not only be happy
But to look forward to tomorrow

* * *

My Mind is in Constant Battle

My mind is in constant battle
With the thoughts inside of my head
Contemplating how to continue living
When I feel as if I am already dead
My emotions overwhelm me and it is getting hard to breathe
Depression has taken over, when will I get relief
I question who I am when I know my soul within
My life is an everyday battle, I know that I can win
I will fight the pessimism that I have let in over the years
'Til I can live the life I love, happy without fear
Depression does not define me
It helps make me who I am
It has given me the strength inside that I never believed I had
I will use that strength to push on forward
and defeat the negative thoughts
So I can begin to find myself
And in life I will no longer feel I am lost

I Know this Life is Testing Me

I know this life is testing me,
and yes, it's for the best
I still can't help but wonder,
when will I pass this test
The ups and downs, the leaps and bounds
That life has thrown my way,
have brought me to this point in time where I'm okay to say
I may be strong, I may be wise, nevertheless naive
Of life itself and how it works
and the steps to becoming complete
Through lifelong struggles and all the hard times
I know deep within, there is a compromise
In the end I've learned and understand
It is not about passing the test
It is about getting through the worst,
only to get to the best

* * *

Take a Deep Breath before the Breakdown

Take a deep breath
before the breakdown
Listen to your heart
when you have no one around
Be conscious of your inner being
and follow in its path
Remember only your heart and soul
can overcome your darkest wrath
Just know the darkness can be forceful
But the light will guide you through
Stay in touch with what you feel
and you will know just what to do.

Strength is Something that Comes from Inside

Strength is something that comes from inside
Not just the muscles but mostly the mind
Its beauty and power help create who you are
Being a delicate flower or a lion with scars
Your strength is what keeps you alive and well
When in times of doubt, never do dwell
Believe in the magic of your own mind
And grow into the bold vibrant flower
Or be the fierce lion with pride

* * *

To Love Yourself is to Free Yourself

To love yourself is to free yourself
Free of all limits and walls
you've built up through the years
Free of all negative and debilitating thoughts
you allow to enter your mind
Just simply let go
Let go of your ego, for none of that is real
You will no longer be held back
from letting your most true self radiate into the world
By freeing yourself, you're allowing your soul
the chance to grow and blossom into love
Love for others but more importantly love for yourself
So be free
and love
above all else

Marla's Story

I "quit" preschool! In Kindergarten, I refused to speak to others or participate in class. I dreaded being called on even though I often knew the answers. This behavior continued for a few decades.

In middle school, I experienced my first panic attack at the podium: racing heart, sweating, shaking, difficulty breathing, and a complete loss of control. My vicious cycle of avoiding any kind of formal or impromptu speaking began when I was a teenager.

My social anxiety improved in high school, thanks to one very special friend who broke me out of my "shell." However, I still avoided presentations and requested to be dropped down an academic level falsely claiming I couldn't handle the workload.

It shouldn't come as a surprise that I majored in Psychology in college. I discovered my diagnosis of Social Anxiety Disorder through a National Anxiety Awareness Day in my second year of college. A few months later, I enrolled in a Cognitive Behavioral Therapy (CBT) group research study for social phobia at Yale. My experience was life changing and my concentration in research was established. Although I made some improvement after participating in that group, my avoidance "strategy" was very time consuming and, ultimately, caused a delay in my graduation twice, both in my undergraduate and graduate degrees.

As would be expected with an anxiety disorder profile of a very high achiever, failure was not an option for me. I earned an A on the one presentation I could not back out of, and I felt I did a great job and hid my anxiety well. What a relief; I thought I was "cured"; until I continued with my avoidance pattern and it caught up with me.

I would get very anxious at staff meetings and events, while being observed interacting with clients, making and receiving phone calls, eating lunch with co-workers, making small talk especially with my supervisors, and the list goes on. Despite the anxiety, or maybe because of it, I worked very hard and managed to get promoted throughout the years. With the increased responsibility in more of a leadership role came more interpersonal interaction, oversight of others, and social situations. Meanwhile, I was going through my graduate program and completely avoiding presentations all over again there and at work, which caused me to seek help.

It took much time and searching to find a place which specialized in anxiety disorders, particularly CBT. Through the process, I accepted social anxiety as a part of me, and the many great qualities attributed to it (yes, I was also shocked upon my revelation of this). However, I knew I also needed a group environment to provide support and structure, and to practice facing my fears in front of support groups.

I began as a member in 2006. Within a year, I was the co-facilitator, then solo facilitator. We met each Saturday morning for three hours for four-month sessions, guided by a program created by the Social Anxiety Institute. This helped me change my irrational thoughts to positive ones and, most importantly, gave me a structured environment to practice behavioral activities (also known as exposures). We also kept each other motivated and accountable to work on our goals between meetings.

In 2009, I created a group, which meets to this day. It is primarily a non-structured group with a mixture of new and continuing members that meets one to two times per month. Each time I meet someone new, I feel a sense of renewal as I witness their first support group experience. These meetings alternate between regular meetings, discussions, and advanced "activity" meetings for behavioral exercises (exposures).

After attending an intense, sixteen-hour weekend workshop (*Getting Over Stage Fright*) in 2010 which directly addressed my fear of public speaking anxiety, my entire mindset changed. I immediately started giving speeches at Toastmasters (after being a member for two years prior without once giving a speech) and took on a leadership and officer role in my new club. The workshop is another example of me transforming from a participant to the facilitator in 2017.

When I met my (now) ex-husband, I had just begun my journey of overcoming Social Anxiety Disorder (SAD). His support led me to a gradual progression of facing more social situations that terrified me. For a few years, I was unable to attend his company parties and be a part of his public career because of the crowds and the scrutiny I felt from everyone. I endured weeks of extreme anxiety leading up to these events. I was convinced I would end up locking myself in the bathroom.

My (now) ex-husband had a knack for challenging me just enough. He proposed to me in front of a large crowd at Disney World, followed by a 12-hour day wearing attention grabbing t-shirts, and a wedding on the beach in Mexico, which was the first time I used a microphone. He would make custom made t-shirts every vacation (usually about my social anxiety) to have me stand out and talk to people. *Hey, I'll raise awareness for social anxiety any way I can; I love it!*

Unfortunately, after 13 years together, we divorced. I felt I had overcome my social and speaking anxiety almost completely. As I approached the dating scene again for the first time in so long, I did have some slight to moderate social anxiety creep back in while dating in the beginning. However, I realized it was nowhere as bad as it once was more than a decade prior because of all the coaching tools I used to help myself. Having social anxiety and dating has been the main topic of many of my support group meetings. It is harder for men as they feel the stereotypical need to make the first moves and be more assertive in public. I plan to form a support group just on this topic alone.

I was curious if my social anxiety would come back to some degree after getting divorced since major life changes sometimes trigger a setback. I was happy to see I was more determined, empowered, and strong to do all the things I needed to do; phone calls, obtaining documents, and managing anxiety in general while going through a different phase of life.

I'm happy to share I felt like a whole new person after the grieving process of divorce. I felt younger and more alive than I had in years and was so excited to spend quality time with friends and experience dating again. I find dating, specifically online dating, intriguing due to my psychological research background; I am simply fascinated and enjoy getting back out there. If only I didn't get divorced during the COVID-19 pandemic, I would have lived life even more fully and traveled more.

I'm able to put things into perspective and keep my thought patterns rational instead of trying to avoid a situation or endure it with a great deal of anxiety. I am constantly aware of the importance of maintaining my progress. It's vital to my growth to continue meeting and (publicly) speaking with new people, nurturing the healing relationships with my fellow anxiety tribe, and keeping a healthy balance between socializing and solitude.

I was scheduled to be a guest speaker at three different networking events for entrepreneurs in the same week! This was in April 2019. Surprisingly, I was barely anxious. In the past, I would have needed a beta-blocker. Taking one didn't cross my mind. I refer to that experience as "new level, new devil", because it was outside my usual groups and workshops. The events went well and I enjoyed the experiences tremendously.

I enjoy coaching one-on-one more than anything. Coaching my passion and no matter what frame of mind I am in personally, I switch to autopilot immediately when it is time to jump on a session or a consultation call. I have a knack for putting pieces together and solving puzzles. Helping someone eliminate debilitating anxiety and self-limited ways of living brings me much joy.

I now live my life with a new outlook, with confidence and energy of which I never dreamed. My experiences have created the person that I am today; the ups and downs and everything in between have served a purpose. As challenging as my journey was, I wouldn't change a thing, it's a part of me.

~Marla Genova, MA
Master Anxiety Coach
CMC Socially Speaking, LLC
marla@sociallyspeakingplus.com
www.socialspeakingplus.com

Nicole's Story

Even though years have passed, I can still remember the moment I was finally given the permission I needed to begin my healing. I was a trained therapist and was sitting on the couch in my new therapist's office, giving her the usual rundown of my life. I gave her my family history; I grew up in North Carolina as the middle child of three girls. My family was Southern Baptist and conservative. I told her about the difficult relationship I had with my mother; I was often the scapegoat for her frustrations and held accountable for my sister's actions even though I had no control over them. I told her about my learning disability and how it had impacted my school career, and the ability to form meaningful relationships.

I shared my ongoing struggle with weight with which I had been diagnosed and derailed by clinical depression and a devastating anxiety disorder in my early adulthood. I disclosed I had been married and divorced three times, and had finally met my person and I didn't want to lose him. He was why I was trying therapy again, this time with a therapist for therapists because I needed an experienced hand to guide me.

She sat quietly and listened. When I was finished, she asked me, "What work have you done to address your trauma?" I became uneasy and replied, "I'm not sure I would go so far as to say that I suffered from trauma." At that moment, I knew I had suffered some abuse, but the word trauma seemed so much bigger. The word trauma seemed so severe, extreme, and beyond what I felt I had a right to call what I'd experienced. That moment changed the direction of my life and healing. There is something powerful in naming an experience so it can be witnessed by a safe person. I will forever be grateful to that therapist.

I have since healed many wounds and have revealed experiences that I know, without a doubt, were trauma. In the moment, even with all the abuse, I realized I did not feel worthy of the term trauma. Isn't that an odd thought, to feel like you need to be worthy of a word? In my mind, until that point, I'd equated trauma with extreme child abuse, domestic violence, rape, murder, and post-traumatic stress disorder (PTSD) from combat experiences. I still did not connect my own experiences with trauma.

My response is not uncommon from people when I bring up the word trauma. People will discount their wounding. The emotionally wounded do not feel as if what happened to them was big enough to be considered traumatizing so they walk around with trauma responses impacting their lives and with no help. By not naming our experiences as trauma, we do nothing to disrupt the stigma that is created by the word trauma and our limited definition of it. I've spent so much time educating people about the many types of trauma and how they impact our lives, our money, and our business.

There are two main classifications of trauma, commonly called "Little T" and "Big T" traumas. "Big T" traumas are events commonly connected with PTSD. The events are shocking, unpredictable experiences causing physical and emotional harm; such as disaster, violence, death, and other crisis situations. Witnessing a "Big T" trauma can cause PTSD. The "Big T" traumas are what most people think of when you say the word trauma, so it makes sense many people wouldn't know that they've experienced trauma.

"Little T" traumas are highly distressing experiences that don't fall into the "Big T" trauma definition. These occurrences are often ongoing and the experience may or may not create a traumatic response for every person. When confronted with "Little T" trauma, a person's support network, resilience, and coping skills can play a huge part in the long-term impact of that trauma.

Here are some examples of "Little T" traumas I see most often. Many of the examples include "Little T" instances which may occur in school including: bullying, neither fitting in nor having a peer group, and undiagnosed and unsupported learning disabilities. Other "Little T" instances may occur at home including, the use of consistent physical punishment in the home, emotional neglect, having divorced parents, going through divorce yourself, moving around often, being a caregiver at a young age, chronic illness, and systems not set up to empower you, but oppress you.

Do you see what I mean by these events? The events are chronic, consistent, and impactful. The events can create wounds that impact thoughts, feelings, and behaviors; which then inform our lives and choices as adults. The events certainly informed mine. I began redefining and naming my experiences, exploring the story I have been telling myself about the experience, and working to change the story by disrupting the pattern.

I have suffered from an undiagnosed learning disability, so every day of school was torture. I thought I was stupid and would never be a success. No one expected me to graduate high school, much less earn a master's degree. My disability changed how I saw myself. It impacted my confidence and I believed for a long time I was not smart, which is not true. In fact, I am considered a thought leader in my field.

I was physically and emotionally abused as a child. These experiences led to feelings of worthlessness, which led to compulsive eating and toxic relationships. For so long, I internalized the abuse as my fault. In fact, it was not my fault, the person abusing me was responding to their own trauma and taking it out on me. Thankfully, I have done some hard work to heal much of my trauma and integrate what I have learned so I can help others do the same. Some of the tools I have used are EFT Tapping, shadow work, and parts work. My "Little T" traumas were impactful on my self-worth. I could not even see the "Big T" traumas when they happened.

I'm thankful for the therapist who opened my eyes and the personal development prompted by my own desire to be successful in my own business. I never imagined starting a business would be a platform from which I could heal a new layer of trauma in my life. I didn't realize starting a business equals entering a relationship and I was about to re-traumatize myself again through my business. Yes, I recreated my trauma in my business, but the good news is I recognized it and flipped the switch.

Instead of my business being a new arena for abuse, I created it to be a platform for healing. Knowledge is power and clarity is key. I am so thankful for all the lessons and how they have become the *why* for my business and my life's work. I now study the impact of childhood trauma on small business owners, entrepreneurs, and leaders. I coach and mentor leaders who want to become more trauma conscious so they can empower their community to grow. When we name something, we can heal it. When we heal it, we can help others. This healing allows us to disrupt the pattern of harm that trauma creates in our lives.

~Nicole Lewis-Keeber, MSW, LCSW
Business Therapist

Joanna's Story

As an intuitive nutrition therapy coach, I have seen transformations beyond nutritional guidance. If we intend to work through our mental health disorders, we need to set the stage so we can heal physically, mentally, emotionally, and spiritually.

Receiving a label of illness is never pleasant. We can choose one of two paths; accept the diagnosis and allow the medical field to medicate us into comfort, or choose to find alternative ways to work through the diagnosis to find who we really are. We can choose to use the diagnosis as the impetus for making needed changes in our lives; changes we may not have made until the pain of the diagnosis challenged us to make lifestyle and perception modifications.

In my 17 years as an intuitive nutrition therapy coach, I have always believed the body has an amazing ability to heal. We just need to use the right tools and learn how to activate our healing ability. Through my own adrenal exhaustion diagnosis over twenty years ago, I experienced this choice first hand. I was a mess. I was wired, tired, and completely depleted. I was at the point where I slept 11 hours per night and still dragged myself through the day, not knowing how I would muster enough energy to get my work done or much of anything else. I felt lost, depressed, and so alone.

I decided to learn about my condition so I could assist my body in repairing itself. The hardest part was working through my own identity. I was an "uber athlete" as my friends called me, I had created an identity based on my athletics. Now I was so exhausted that I wasn't sure who I was. Surely, I wasn't an athlete; not in those initial moments.

I worked with a nutritionist who introduced me to vegetable juicing, a liquid IV of nutrients. I learned how to balance my blood sugar and not use the standard athlete diet, which was heavily carbohydrate-based and highly inflammatory. As my blood sugar balanced, my moods, my outlook, and my view of who I was improved. I adapted my food choices based on what it was my body needed and continued this for many years, trying new combinations and recipes to determine what was best for my body and my brain. I let go of what others thought was "the solution" and found combinations that worked for me.

The diagnosis played with my head. I had to really connect with what it was I loved; not what others thought I should do, but what I loved to do what brought *me* joy. I discovered yoga which was calming to my mind and I realized that exercise was my way of meditating. Exercise was when I felt most connected to myself and God. I could find the answers to anything when I moved. My mind was calm and my body felt grounded. My body loved to move, yet I needed to move the way my body needed on that day. To this day, I still move my body every day because it makes my body and mind feel alive.

I had to really look at myself in the mirror and start loving who it was that I was admiring. Others could see my beauty, but I could not see it. Maybe all the years of criticism from family had created the worst critic of all; me against myself.

Initially, I was so full of self-loathing, all I could see were all my flaws my thunder thighs, my cellulite, and the dark circles under my eyes. To the outsider, I was fit, attractive, and successful. To me, I was none of those things. I had lost the ability to see beauty; the beauty all around me and the beauty of me. Using food as medicine was much easier than this idea of self-love. As I focused on what brought me joy, I started to see beauty in situations rather than seeing the darkness of a challenge. It was hard to be nice to myself and I worked on reframing my language towards myself. Looking back, I often felt betrayed; I realize now, it was me betraying myself. Others were just mirroring my own feelings against me. As I learned to see myself as my best friends would see me, I was able to change my perception of me and really love who I am. I let go of who others thought I should be. I stopped trying to live up to their ideals. My loving ideals became my motivation. As my self-love grew, self-criticism and criticism from family ceased. In truth, my family just wanted me to be happy. I can see now that the criticism was just a means to inspire me to take a stand on what I believed in. Once I chose me and self-love, I received the love and support I wanted.

With my clients, I encourage them to find the activities which bring them joy. Anything; walking in the woods or by a body of water, painting, dancing, cooking, or other creative outlets. If you are someone who has been squelched because of your diagnosis, I encourage you to choose one thing you love to do every day. This behavior will improve how you feel about yourself and your circumstance more than you know.

I encourage you to look at how you eat and what you eat. As you take an honest inventory, start noticing how you feel after you eat certain foods or meals. Do those foods increase or decrease your energy? Does your body feel good or heavy and bogged down? Are you stress eating? If so, what is the trigger and can you work through the trigger or find a healthier alternative?

If you start a food journal, you can start to track what you have eaten, how you feel before and after the meals, and how your food choices are affecting your well-being. Start choosing more nutrient-dense foods. Start cooking one meal per day at home and adding more calmness and enjoyment to your meals. Be kind to yourself no matter what you are choosing to eat. You are doing the best you can at this moment.

Stress management is a lifelong commitment to developing a lens of compassion, love, and understanding for yourself, your situation, and others. I had to learn how to love myself and take care of me, myself, and I. I worked through books and exercises to help me become a better communicator who could express my feelings with compassion rather than react from feeling hurt.

I work with clients to set the stage for their own healing journey. We first improve their nutrition so their body is nourished with nutrient dense foods which feed their brain and body. We find movement and activities that bring them joy. We find time to play, time to regenerate, and time to recover in peaceful settings. We work through situations and triggers with peace, love, and understanding of who they are. We activate their skill of listening to what their body, mind, and soul need at every moment.

Everyone has his or her own journey. I have mine and will continue to assist others in making their journey more loving to their whole body by reframing challenges into opportunities for adventure to give their life more joy. Together we set the stage so the body, mind, and soul can heal. As they heal, they embrace and embody who they are and see the goodness their life has offered through a lens of love.

~Joanna Chodorowska
Holistic Nutritionist
Body in Motion
joanna@n-im.net

Sharon's Spirituality Insight

What does spirituality mean to you as you see it? The definition of spirituality is "the quality of being concerned with the human spirit or soul as opposed to material or physical things."[6] To answer the question, to me spirituality is real. It has become my whole focus. I like to call it "the point of light." The mindfulness part of this, for me, is to remain in "love consciousness" or simply put, *kindness.* I feel my spiritual focus has left me open and vulnerable to healthy, growth, no matter how difficult it seems.

Remembering to breathe well (softly and deeply), is number one in achieving positive healthy growth. The mind will easily go south if this breathing (softly and deeply) is paused for even the shortest period. Know that shallow breathing changes your level of frequency. This is very important, yet easily remedied. If we find ourselves not breathing softly and deeply, we can notice and start again. Easy, right? Experts have said if we were to focus on our breathing for one solid hour, we would become enlightened.

Not allowing judgment to take over the mind is key to truthful and accurate perception. We are all biased, so just listening to initial judgment and allowing our perception to be valid is enough to move past it and onto what is true. By moving past judgment, we are less charged emotionally and can heal readily or learn more.

---

[6] "Definition of spirituality". Lexico. December 2020. Oxford University Press. https://www.lexico.com/en/definition/spirituality (accessed December 13, 2020).

I have created a positive focus on learning, experiencing spirit, and becoming kinder and wiser. The journey is the path of spirituality. It is going to feel like a roller-coaster ride with great ups and downs when we have traumas in our pasts, which is perfectly normal. My own experience with the path of spirituality has been one of wise kindness. The truth matters to me. Positive momentum and experience keep me in this game. It's okay to be a beginner, it's okay to be proficient. Your level will change according to each moment and new experience.

In the hope of making real progress in all of this, I knew inherently meditation would be the most effective technique. Sound healing became the way of nurture and ease for real solid help. Sound healing therapy creates more vibration and less matter, and cleanses feelings and emotion. The therapy helps so much more than analyzing and getting stuck in the muck of mind traps. Sound healing therapy is done with frequency, musical notes, melody, and stimulation. Crystal singing bowls, metal singing bowls, alchemy singing bowls, tuning forks, crystals, Trinfinity8, drums, and other sound healing tools are my way to help myself, my family, my friends, and my clients feel better and stay on their own path of positive focus and growth. This experience has made my life incredibly rewarding, far more than money or physical fitness could.

Bringing the heart of spirituality into the physical and monetary world has been challenging but rewarding to my growth. I could never abandon the beauty of this commitment for myself and others. I enjoy this path; watching it unfold for others is so sweet.

I've had success in my heart, which has made all the difference to my soul. As a mom, a wife, sister, a friend to many and a ceremony officiating Interfaith Minister, I provide Sound Healing with Angelic Reiki and Trinfinity 8 classes and individual sessions, Angelic Reiki Attunements one on one. I also offer house cleansing with blessings and private parties! I offer individual Sessions include Angelic Reiki, Sound Healing & Trinfinity 8: A Trinity of Modalities! I welcome you to try sound healing at Attuned with Spirit located at 1454 Bethlehem Pike in North Wales, Pennsylvania.

~Reverend Sharon Kachel
Attuned with Spirit
Angelic Reiki Master
Sound Healing Therapy
Meditation Teacher
Spiritual Coach
Meditations and Ceremonies
Property Clearing and Blessing
attunedwithspirit@gmail.com
https://www.attunedwithspirit.com/

~Wisdom from Yanni~

- Meditation teaches you how to be present.
- Stop trying so hard with your mind to find your purpose in life. It will get you nowhere. It will only exhaust you. Instead, still your mind, go within, listen to that *still small voice within*, and experience the inherent wholeness which is at your core. There you will find the true meaning and purpose of your life.
- Be very mindful about who and what you invite into your internal dialogues. It has a profound impact on your life. When you invite anger, you experience anger. When you invite fear, you experience fear. When you invite worry, you experience worry. On the other hand, when you invite joy, you experience joy. When you invite peace, you experience peace. When you invite love, you experience love.
- The kinds of thoughts you choose are like the kinds of friends you choose. Who you hang out with determines who you bring home with you which determines the quality of your life.
- If I follow anyone other than myself, I will surely get lost.
- True self-confidence is having the courage to listen to the *still small voice within* and act on its inspirations and promptings.
- Only meditation can open the door to our inner treasure, fortune, and inheritance and help reveal to us our true nature.
- Meditation is when you are focused on just what *is* and when you are just *being present*; yes, just *being present*.
- Are you here in the now or are you thinking about a whole bunch of different things, past and future? Are you multi-tasking, multi-thinking, and multi-doing? Or *just feeling*? Where are you? Are you here? There is only here. There is only now.
- Peace of mind is a thought away, an image away, a breath away.
- Shift out of your mind and enter the land of your soul; there you will know who you are, where you are, where you are going, and what to do.
- Literally, with one deep breath, with one thought other than the chain of negative thoughts you've got flying through your brain, or with one positive image, you can switch gears. You can literally *change your mind* and change what you are experiencing.

- You don't need to create a life script to follow, it has all been sketched out for you. Your job is to discover, recover, uncover, and then follow it. That is what *following your bliss* is all about.
- Constantly keep focusing away from the negative *stuff* and, instead, ask to see *good* in any given situation. As well, honor other people's journeys rather than judging them. Appreciate and accept everyone and everything with *gratitude* and always ask yourself, what did this situation or individual teach me? Then sit back and listen for the answer.
- Listen to your intuition instead of over-planning, all you need to do is "tune in" to what is the next *first step* and then take it.
- Ask yourself now and reflect on whether you live in the shadows of your ego's limitations and illusions or the brilliant *light of your soul.*
- Every tense thought creates tension in your body. Every peaceful thought creates peace in your body and your life.
- Connecting intuitively is an effortless process, one for which there is no mental effort or striving, rather a flow of the *Divine* to us and our thoughts.
- Intuition is being present with yourself. It is found in the silence. It is found in your heart.
- Intuition assumes nothing, it just knows. It is a process. It is always changing. It is never the same.
- Abundance is not a possession; it is a state of mind.
- Keep asking yourself moment to moment: Does this present thought have compassion? Does this present feeling have empathy? Does this present path have a heart? Does this present action heal? How near to silence are my words? Is my mind presently at peace? Nothing else matters.
- Dare to trust what you receive intuitively.

~Yanni Maniates
Author/Lecturer
Intuitive Development and Meditation Teacher
Global Projects @ Unity Earth

~Wellness Tools~

Activity-Be active even on your laziest days! Do a quick workout, go for a walk, play a sport, take an exercise class. Moving your body and, more importantly, breaking a sweat can help release endorphins and serotonin which play an important part in regulating your mood.

Books and Speakers-Even if you only have time for a few pages, it can help shift your mindset. Self-help books have lifted me out of many dark times because I was able to relate to what I was reading. Some of my favorite inspirational speakers are: Brené Brown, Les Brown, Joe Dispenza, Wayne Dyer, and Tony Robbins.

Creativity-Let your creativity run free. Many creative activities like painting, drawing, crafting, wood working, jewelry making, photography, music making, calligraphy, dancing, knitting, cross stitching, crocheting, embroidery, baking, cooking, etc. are also very relaxing and give your mind something positive and beautiful to focus on. Play games or do a puzzle.

Diagnosis-Educate yourself about the signs and symptoms. Putting a name to these things gives you power over them. If you have been prescribed medication, take it as directed by your doctor.

Electronics-Limit TV, Internet, and Social Media-Although there are plenty of positive and uplifting influences, there are just as many negative. Sometimes getting sucked into the media can unknowingly affect your mindset and your outlook on yourself and the world.

Essential Oils and Healing Crystals-These are tools you can use throughout your home and daily life to encourage positive energy and wellness.

Experiences-Stepping out of what is familiar can be a daunting task. Once you do it, you may find that it could change not only your mood but also your life! Whether you try something you have never done or do something you've always wanted to do but have never had the courage for; take that leap! You will not regret it!

Gratitude-First thing in the morning and last thing before bed, remind yourself of what you are grateful for in life!

Journaling-Keep a journal with you wherever you go. Take time to sit down and write. Get your feelings out on paper. Doing so will help you make sense of them. Alternatively, write letters to friends and family. Send inspirational and affirmational cards to those who may need to be uplifted. Send cards to family and friends for important dates and holidays.

Love-Remember there is always room in your heart for love, for not only others but yourself.

Meditation-Sit and focus on your breath. If your mind begins to wander, try using a mantra. My go-to mantra is "Out of the mind, and into the heart." Saying a mantra repeatedly will guide you into quieting your mind and body. Meditation helps with thought awareness and introspection. Meditation can provide relief for stress, anxiety, depression, physical pain, ruminating thoughts, and PTSD flashbacks.

Mindfulness-Be fully aware of a situation or the thoughts that enter your brain. If the situation or thoughts are negative or self-sabotaging, notice them and replace that situation or those thoughts with something positive. Practice positive self-talk. Take time to pray. Light candles; use them to signal quiet time for yourself.

Music-Listen to music that makes you smile or feel good inside. Singing along gives me an extra boost of enjoyment. Soothing music helps calm you. Try some of these artists: Enya, Joanne Shenandoah, David Young, and Yanni. Natural white noise can also provide relief. Take a bubble bath and listen to your favorite music.

Nature-Whether it's for a walk, a run, or simply a chance to sit in the grass by a tree or creek; get out into nature. Listen to your surroundings for things as simple as a bird chirping. These sounds can bring you a glimpse of happiness. Visit the beach. Watch a sunset or sunrise. Take pictures in nature with family, friends, or pets. Plant a garden; flowers, herbs, or produce. Use a pot in your house if you do not have a yard.

Nutrition-What you put in your body can affect your mental, emotional, and physical well-being. Yes, sometimes you just need that pint of ice cream! Do not beat yourself up for it and don't make it an unhealthy habit. Look into how the chemicals in food can affect the chemicals in your brain. Your mind and gut are more connected than you could imagine!

Professional Support-Talking to someone about what you're going through whether it be good or bad can help tremendously. I highly suggest finding a therapist who you can connect with. Yes, talking to a trusted friend or family member is great, but a professional can give you tools and advice that have helped many others with similar struggles.

Salt Spa Treatments-These treatments relieve stress, anxiety, and depression. They also rid your body of positive ions from electronics and replace those ions in your body with negative ions which help heal ailments. Salt can also provide respiratory relief for allergies, asthma, or bronchial issues.

Smile-This may seem silly but I've tried it and it works! If you're feeling down and cannot think of a reason to smile, simply force yourself to smile! It naturally releases good, healthy chemicals in your brain such as: dopamine, serotonin, oxytocin, and endorphine, all chemicals which relieve stress, ease depression, and soothe anxiety.

Sound Healing-Use drums, singing bowls, bells, tuning forks, gongs, and rain sticks, to help heal you mentally, emotionally, physically, and spiritually. Sound healing raises your vibration.

Substance Use-AVOID-Drugs and alcohol may feel like they help in the moment but they will only lead to more problems and more trauma in the long run.

Support-Go to a class or event where people support and empower one another. Consider becoming a Peer Support Specialist to be a supportive influence for someone else.

Variation in Routine-Make your bed each morning. Take a shower. Put on a nice outfit; add make up or cologne. Try a new hairstyle, get a haircut. Buy a new outfit or new shoes. Rearrange your living room. Decorate for the holidays.

Yoga-This is a gentle and sometimes vigorous way of moving your body in flow with your breath to help relax your mind.

~Rachel Ellis
~Maggie Catagnus

Ah, Mania!

You are faithful, I'll give you that,
coming 'round just in time for Valentine's Day.
You snuggle close and ask me to be yours.
I smile knowingly, and say,
Show me your virtues... if you have any.
You, in the guise of a gypsy,
with pots and pans strung across your back,
take down a few tarnished wares and hold them out to me.
I snort. Haven't we been through all this before?
Then, as I touch your roughed cheek,
I ask, why won't you give me up?
What am I to you?
Your gypsy eyes, ringed with soot, brush my face.
Okay, I say, it was good. I admit it.
I saw the stars with you.
We ran with the moon at our backs,
leaped across the sleeping earth.
You showed me the future
in a dead dog's eye, then led me away
lest I drown in my own dream.
You spun sweet songs from the morning breeze
and trickled them through my hair.
You peeled back the world so I could dip inside.
Took the fire from the sun
and winked it in my heart.
Okay, I say, You're a marvel,
a regular storehouse of miracles.
But can't we say goodbye?
It's February and you've come back.
You always do.
I hear you breathing at my front door, soft as a kitten.
I'd know that sound anywhere.
Let me in, let me in, you whimper.
Can't you be more original?
Once I followed you
blissfully
blindly

Never dreaming of deceit,
dazed by your taste for light and color
awed by your contempt of boundaries
so like my own
which you swept away
with a lion's paw
while I cheered you on from the sidelines,
until I found myself
tethered
insensate
to a hospital bed.
And forgot I had a name.
Amid the tumult,
amid the sea of screams,
the broken minds a-bob the
slicing waves like so many
wind-up clocks jangling out of time,
who should come 'round but you.
Fancy!
There, amid the black,
the granite slab of eternity sawing through my chest,
Your shadow on the wall.
You kissed my eyes
and bid me see.
Ah, Mania,
My debt to you is incalculable,
simply beyond measure,
But no pots and pans today,
Dear Gypsy,
Put them away.
Today I shall travel the world alone.
Fishing for words,
as I do.
The
search
sans you.

~Ruth Z. Deming

~Inspiration from My Journey~

- Rise above the noise and fly, baby, fly!
- Relax, unwind, we are all in this together.
- Go within yourself and be amazed by what you find.
- Open your mind and you will see.
- True beauty comes from within.
- Being honest with yourself is freedom.
- Don't forget you are a *warrior*! Keep fighting. Never give up.
- What may look like a failure can be a moment to grow. Keep trying, this moment made you who you are today.
- This too shall pass.
- Forgiveness is everlasting.
- Live your greatest truth.
- I am on my next step to my healing.
- I am taking responsibility for my own actions. No blame.
- I am aware there are many things I can do to change.
- I am on an ever-changing journey.
- Face difficult days by saying, "Thank you, mental health challenge, I am who I am today because of you. You taught me a lot and I am forever grateful."
- Life is not perfect for any person. You may exclaim; "Why me? What did I do to deserve this? How can life be so cruel?" In these moments, remember that everyone has problems, painful experiences, disappointments, chaos, overwhelming feelings, heartache, and suffering. It takes a village; help one another.
- Challenges can be looked at as opportunities to learn and try out new behaviors.
- Think about how you are going to protect yourself emotionally from a toxic person. Their negative energy will bring you down.
- Remember you are not crazy and you are not alone. Many people have struggles. Hundreds of thousands of people are living proof recovery happens and you can lead a productive life.
- When you feel considerable pain and suffering because of your mental health, respond to the pain of someone else's struggles. It's

a good feeling to help someone else. Helping someone else takes the focus off your pain (be mindful of whether you are well enough to reach out to someone).

- You are a *warrior* and *survivor*! You will get through this. Think back to other struggling times. Remember you made it through. Remember you cannot do it alone.
- Make helping others a priority. It will give you enormous satisfaction, especially when you are struggling (be mindful of whether you have the strength to help others).
- The more you give and show kindness, the more you will get; the Law of Attraction.
- Your expectations of others can sometimes disappoint you.
- Be a positive example for someone.
- Strive for emotional and spiritual balance.
- It's okay to ask for help. We all need help from time to time. Reaching out for help is courageous.
- Let life unfold naturally. **Flow**.
- The Time is Right. The Time is Now. *Feel It, Heal It, Let It Go!*

~Biblical Passage~

And the angel said unto them,
Fear not: for, behold, I bring you good tidings
of great joy, which shall be to all people.
For unto you is born this day in the city of David
a Savior, who is Christ the Lord.
And this shall be a sign unto you,
You shall find
the baby wrapped in swaddling clothes,
laying in a manger.
And suddenly there was with the angel
a multitude of the heavenly host
praising God, and saying,
"Glory to God in the highest,
and on earth peace, good will toward men."

~Luke 2:10-14

When you're in a situation, ask yourself,
"What would Jesus do?"

* * *

We miss you, Mama.
We know you are our angel
and are always with us.
Peace and love to all!

* * * *Rest in Peace, Robin Williams** * *

~Resources~

Suicide Prevention

Substance Abuse and Mental Health Services Administration (SAMHSA) provides suicide prevention information and other resources for behavioral health professionals, the public, and people at risk. **If you need help now, please call 911 or contact SAMHSA's National Suicide Prevention Lifeline (https://suicidepreventionlifeline.org/) at 1-800-273-TALK (8255).**

SAMHSA is a partner of the National Action Alliance for Suicide Prevention (http://actionallianceforsuicideprevention.org/), a public-private partnership advancing the national strategy for suicide prevention. Suicide is a serious public health problem that causes immeasurable pain, suffering, and loss to individuals, families, and communities nationwide.

Suicide prevention efforts seek to:
- Reduce factors to increase the risk for suicidal thoughts and behaviors.
- Increase the factors that help strengthen, support, and protect individuals from suicide.

Ideally, the efforts listed above address individual, relationship, community, and societal factors. The efforts are designed to promote hope, ease access into effective treatment, encourage connectedness, and support recovery.

The causes of suicide are complex and determined by multiple combinations of factors, such as mental illness, substance abuse, painful losses, exposure to violence, and social isolation.

Warning signs which may mean someone is at risk include:
- Talking about wanting to die or kill oneself
- Looking for a way to kill oneself
- Talking about feeling hopeless or having no reason to live
- Talking about feeling trapped or being in unbearable pain
- Talking about being a burden to others

- Increasing the use of alcohol or drugs
- Acting anxious or agitated; behaving recklessly
- Sleeping too little or too much
- Withdrawing or feeling isolated
- Showing rage or talking about seeking revenge
- Displaying extreme mood swings

The risk is greater if the behavior is new, or has increased, and if it seems related to a painful event, loss, or change.

If you believe someone may be contemplating suicide:
- Call 911, if danger of self-harm seems imminent.
- Ask if he or she is having suicidal thoughts. (NOTE: Asking this question will NOT put thoughts into their head or increase the likelihood of a suicide attempt.)
- Listen without judging and show you care.
- Stay with the person (or make sure the person is in a private, secure place with another caring person) until you can get help.
- Remove any objects which could be used in a suicide attempt.
- Call SAMHSA's National Suicide Prevention Lifeline at 1-800-273-TALK (8255) and follow their guidance.

Everyone has a role in preventing suicide. Faith communities work to prevent suicide by fostering life-preserving cultures and norms, and providing perspective and social support to community members. Community members can help struggling people navigate life to find a sustainable sense of hope, meaning, and purpose.

Although a prior suicide attempt is one of the strongest risk factors for suicide, nine in 10 do not ultimately die by suicide. People who have lived through suicidal experiences are writing and speaking about their experiences, connecting with one another, and sharing their pathways to wellness and recovery. The Action Alliance's *The Way Forward.* (https://theactionalliance.org/resource/way-forward-pathways-hope-recovery-and-wellness-insights-lived-experience)

Losing a loved one to suicide is painful for family members and friends. SAMHSA's Suicide Prevention Resource Center (http://www.sprc.org/) helps loss survivors find local and national organizations, websites, and other resources providing support, healing, and a sense of community (http://www.sprc.org/basics/about-surviving-suicide-loss). https://www.samhsa.gov/find-help/suicide-prevention [7]

NAMI Peer-to-Peer

NAMI Peer-to-Peer is a free, eight-session educational program for adults with mental health conditions who are looking to better understand themselves and their recovery. Taught by trained leaders with lived experience, this program includes activities, discussions and informative videos. However, as with all NAMI programs, it does not include recommendations for treatment approaches.

NAMI Peer-to-Peer is a safe, confidential space. The course provides an opportunity for mutual support and growth. Experience compassion and understanding from people who relate to your experiences. NAMI is a place to learn more about recovery in an accepting environment.

NAMI Peer-to-Peer helps you:

- Set a vision and goals for the future
- Partner with health care providers
- Develop confidence for making decisions
- Practice relaxation and stress reduction tools
- Share your story
- Strengthen relationships
- Enhance communication skills
- Learn about mental health treatment options

NAMI Connection

NAMI Connection is a weekly recovery support group for people living with mental illness in which people learn from each other's experiences, share coping strategies, and offer each other encouragement and understanding. NAMI Family Support Group

---

[7] Substance Abuse and Mental Health Services Administration, "Suicide Prevention," SAMHSA, accessed January 4, 2021, https://www.samhsa.gov/find-help/suicide-prevention

(https://nami.org/Support-Education/Support-Groups/NAMI-Family-Support-Group) is a support group for family members, significant others and friends of people with mental health conditions. Groups meet weekly, every other week or monthly, depending on location.

Across the country, thousands of trained NAMI volunteers bring peer-led programs to numerous community settings, from churches to schools to NAMI Affiliates. With the unique understanding of people with lived experience, programs and support groups provide outstanding free education, skills training and support.

NAMI Education Classes
NAMI Basics (https://nami.org/Support-Education/Mental-Health-Education/NAMI-Basics)
NAMI Basics is a class for parents, guardians and other family caregivers who provide care for youth (age 22 or younger) who are experiencing mental health symptoms.

NAMI Family-to-Family (https://nami.org/Support-Education/Mental-Health-Education/NAMI-Family-to-Family)
NAMI Family-to-Family is a class for families, significant others and friends of people with mental health conditions. Designated as an evidence-based program by SAMHSA, the teachers of the class facilitate a better understanding of mental health conditions, increase coping skills and empower participants to become advocates for their family.

NAMI Homefront (https://nami.org/Support-Education/Mental-Health-Education/NAMI-Homefront)
NAMI Homefront is a class for families, caregivers and friends of military service members and veterans with mental health conditions. The course is designed specifically to help these families understand those challenges and improve their ability to support their service member or veteran.
(https://www.nami.org/Support-Education/Mental-Health-Education/NAMI-Peer-to-Peer)
~Namaste~

Made in USA - Kendallville, IN
43256_9781736770207
03.29.2022 1505